2

SUSTAINABLE AGRICULTURE

▲ by Carol Hand

Content Consultant

Chad Kruger
Director of the Center for Sustaining Agriculture &
Natural Resources
Washington State University

Essential Library

An Imprint of Abdo Publishing | abdopublishing.com

CUTTING EDGE
SCIENCE +
TECHNOLOGY

abdopublishing.com

Published by Abdo Publishing, a division of ABDO, PO Box 398166, Minneapolis, Minnesota 55439. Copyright © 2016 by Abdo Consulting Group, Inc. International copyrights reserved in all countries. No part of this book may be reproduced in any form without written permission from the publisher. Essential Library™ is a trademark and logo of Abdo Publishing.

Printed in the United States of America, North Mankato, Minnesota
092015
012016

THIS BOOK CONTAINS
RECYCLED MATERIALS

Cover Photo: iStockphoto
Interior Photos: Robert Polett/AgStock Images/Corbis, 4–5; Yasushi Kanno/The Yomiuri Shimbun/AP Images, 7; Roberto E. Rosales/ZumaPress/Corbis, 9; Vladislav Gajic/Shutterstock Images, 11; Adam Stoltman/Corbis, 13; Brent Winebrenner/Getty Images, 14–15; iStockphoto, 17, 19, 27, 39, 41, 70, 80, 86–87, 98; David Hughes/iStockphoto, 22; Gleb Stock/Shutterstock Images, 23; Robert George Young/Masterfile/Corbis, 24–25; Jonathan Woodcock/iStockphoto, 28; Surachet Khamsuk/Shutterstock Images, 33; Co Rentmeester/The LIFE Picture Collection/Getty Images , 35; Ahmed Jallanzo/EPA/Corbis, 36–37; Bettmann/Corbis, 43; Paulo Fridman/Bloomberg/Getty Images, 46; Rodger Bosch/AFP/Getty Images, 49; Gosia Wozniacka/AP Images, 50–51; Jim Richardson/National Geographic Creative/Corbis, 53; Charlie Riedel/AP Images, 55; Tammy Ljungblad/MCT/Newscom, 59; Kiichiro Sato/AP Images, 61; Rich Pedroncelli/AP Images, 62–63; George Burba/Getty Images, 65; Dan Ogle/USDA Natural Resources Conservation Service, 69; Red Line Editorial, 72; NASA/GSFC/METI/Japan Space Systems, 73; Shutterstock Images, 74–75, 85, 95; Digital Vision/Photodisc/Thinkstock, 77; Forward Thinking Architecture - Aerial side view of a cluster formed of SFF modules, 89; Micah Youello/iStockphoto, 91; Wally Eberhart/Visuals Unlimited/Corbis, 93

Editor: Nick Rebman
Series Designer: Craig Hinton

Library of Congress Control Number: 2015945641

Cataloging-in-Publication Data
Hand, Carol.
 Sustainable agriculture / Carol Hand.
   p. cm. -- (Cutting-edge science and technology)
 ISBN 978-1-62403-919-5 (lib. bdg.)
 Includes bibliographical references and index.
 1. Sustainable agriculture --Juvenile literature.   I. Title.
 631.5--dc23

                                                            2015945641

CONTENTS

ONE

DEFINING SUSTAINABLE AGRICULTURE

In agriculture, less is sometimes more. Just ask ranchers Dan and Jeanne Carver, owners of the Imperial Stock Ranch in Shaniko, Oregon. On their 30,000 acres (12,000 ha) of rangeland, the Carvers raise 600 cattle and 240 ewes per year. The Carvers make a good living from their ranch. But one of their major goals is to rejuvenate the land, which was badly eroded and compacted when they bought the property in 1988. Soil had also washed into the ranch's streams, destroying the trout habitat. They rejuvenate the land by taking care of the soil—largely by leaving it alone and letting nature take its course. For example, they use no-till farming on their 3,000 acres (1,200 ha) of grain. In no-till farming, the soil is not turned over with a plow or disk. Rather, seed is drilled directly into the ground, through the residue of previous years' crops. Growing grain without

A tractor with a no-till drill plants soybeans in Iowa.

5

tilling the soil helps the Carvers, too. It saves them $20,000 per year in fuel costs, and the crop residue saves them $40,000 per year in calf feed.[1]

To maintain the rangeland, they practice a technique known as intensive grazing management. They graze each of the ranch's 70 fenced pastures no more than three weeks per year. In addition to constructing fences to control where the stock goes, they built watering holes to keep their cattle from further damaging the ranch's 150 miles (240 km) of streams. These methods promote grass growth and protect riparian, or riverbank, areas. Since implementing these techniques, steelhead trout have made a comeback, and beef production has tripled. Ron Carver is not surprised. "I like the concept of conservation," he says. "I've seen the results of 100 years of doing it the wrong way. Every time you do something with your livestock, you should be thinking about the health of the land."[2]

The Carvers certainly use modern technology as needed, but they do not rely on flashy equipment. They use brainpower, common sense, and a deep understanding of farm and rangeland ecology. Their approach is called sustainable agriculture, and it can be applied to any type of farm. Take, for example, Don Bustos of Santa Cruz Farm in New Mexico. Bustos has also been farming since the 1980s, when he took over the struggling farm his family has owned for 300 years.

Small but Sustainable

Bustos owns only 3.5 acres (1.4 ha) of land, along with 10,000 square feet (930 sq m) of greenhouses. He has organic certification, which proves his farm meets United States Department of Agriculture (USDA) regulations for organic food production. He produces 72 different fruit and vegetable crops year-round, including asparagus, blackberries, and strawberries. Bustos's sustainable farming methods are a mixture of old and new. The solar panels he installed in 2005 cut his greenhouse heating costs

A worker harvests lettuce in a greenhouse whose electricity comes from solar power.

from $2,000 per year to zero, enabling him to grow salad greens all year; this increased his yields by 30 to 40 percent.[3] Water conservation is vital in dry New Mexico. Bustos uses mulches to conserve water and prevent erosion, and he is a member of an *acequia*, or community-owned drip irrigation project.

To overcome poor soil fertility, Bustos practices a number of techniques. First, he uses intensive crop rotation. He also plants cover crops, which are crops grown specifically to protect and benefit the soil rather than for sale. In addition, Bustos uses mulches made with organic alfalfa hay. This material

An acequia in New Mexico delivers water to crops.

is high in nitrogen, an element that is particularly important for helping plants grow. Finally, Bustos uses integrated pest management strategies. He provides habitat for beneficial insects, which are those that provide functions such as pest control and pollination. He also schedules planting for times when crops are least likely to be harmed by pests.

Bustos says, "Little farms can make a big impact if they get their techniques down."[4] His farm and his life are models of sustainable agriculture, showing how economic, ecological, and social values interact in this developing field. Bustos markets directly to restaurants and schools. He works hard to sell his crops, getting them to market quickly while they are still fresh. He helped build a permanent farmers' market in Santa Fe and helps run two community-supported agriculture (CSA) programs, which sell food directly to families. Bustos also works with youth programs to encourage the next generation of farmers, and he participates in a national initiative to help immigrants and economically disadvantaged populations.

Acequias for Water Sharing

Acequias, or communal irrigation systems, have sustained agriculture in New Mexico's arid climate for the past four centuries, since Spanish settlers brought them to North America. The acequia is a way of conserving and sharing water, which Indo-Hispanos view as a communal resource. Acequia members assemble annually to clean out the *acequia madre*, or mother ditch—the canal from which all members receive irrigation water. A *mayordomo*, or water master, decides water distribution among acequia members, with members' consent. He or she monitors water flow and assigns each member a time each week to irrigate his or her fields.

◢ Origin of the TBL

John Elkington, founder of the British consulting group SustainAbility, coined the phrase *triple bottom line* in 1994. He wanted companies to consider three separate bottom lines rather than only the one related to economic profit. He defined the second as the "people account," measuring the company's social responsibility, and the third as the "planet account," measuring its environmental responsibility. Only then, Elkington said, was a company considering the full cost of doing business. Social costs became more obvious when companies such as Nike were caught using child labor in less-developed countries. Environmental damage, including carbon pollution and rainforest logging, also helped spur the TBL movement. But the people and planet aspects of TBL are hard to measure. Most companies still focus on profit as the only bottom line.

What Is Sustainable Agriculture?

The USDA's definition of sustainable agriculture comes from John Ikerd of the University of Missouri. Ikerd defined sustainable agriculture as farming systems "capable of maintaining their productivity and usefulness to society indefinitely. Such systems . . . must be resource-conserving, socially supportive, commercially competitive, and environmentally sound."[5]

In 1987, the Brundtland Commission of the United Nations defined the term *sustainable* to mean agriculture must meet present needs while still making it possible for future generations to meet their needs. This requires us to be stewards of both natural and human resources. It also requires an interdisciplinary approach throughout the entire food system. That is, all interested parties—researchers, farmers, farmworkers, consumers, and politicians—must cooperate to make sustainable agriculture work. Sustainable agriculture incorporates three separate but interrelated goals: economic profitability, social equity, and environmental health. In the sustainability movement, these goals are referred to as the triple bottom line (TBL). They are also described as the three Ps: profit, people, and planet.

The Three Legs of Sustainability

The Center for Integrated Agricultural Systems (CIAS) at the University of Wisconsin illustrates sustainable agriculture as a three-legged stool. All three legs—representing the economy, environment, and community— are necessary for agricultural systems to remain stable and sustainable.

Sustainability Combines Old and New

When most people think of cutting-edge science and technology, they envision shiny, exciting inventions—perhaps a self-driving car or a single pill that cures cancer. Sustainable agriculture sometimes appears to take the opposite approach, with people returning to old methods rather than looking forward. There is good reason for this. Some advances in agriculture seemed miraculous in the 1940s and 1950s; for example, pesticides destroyed harmful insects, and artificial fertilizers combined

with improved genetics dramatically increased crop production. But few people in the industry or society considered potential negative effects of these technologies. Now, as people observe these harmful effects, many are beginning to take a different approach toward the use of technology in agriculture.

Wind turbines provide farmers with renewable energy.

Nevertheless, today's sustainable farmers are not turning away from technology. Instead, they consider farming from a broader perspective. They are seeking new directions, using science-based methods and technology so they lead to sustainability rather than the destruction of the environment. As farmers begin to consider profit, people, and planet instead of profit alone, they may sometimes return to tried-and-true methods, in which they step back and let nature take its course. But sustainable farmers also move forward, developing new technologies and adapting old ones to better meet the goals of sustainability. These technological advances include more efficient farm equipment, applications of alternative energy, use of biotechnology, and use of electronic systems such as global positioning systems (GPS). Sustainable farmers hope that, with proper care and application, these new techniques and technologies will nurture many future generations.

TWO

WHY WE NEED SUSTAINABLE AGRICULTURE

In the 1930s and 1940s, British botanist Sir Albert Howard was in India learning sustainable agricultural techniques. But in the developed world, most agricultural experts were moving in the opposite direction—toward highly chemical, technological solutions to increasing crop production. Many people today would say the technological approach was highly successful. A walk through any American supermarket reveals a huge, varied, and nutritious food supply. So, why do we need sustainable agriculture? We need it because, under the surface, modern industrial agriculture has major shortcomings; many of its technologies and practices are not sustainable. According to John Ikerd, retired professor of agriculture from the University of Missouri, ecological, social, and economic problems in today's food production system require a switch to

A farm worker uses a simple irrigation system in India.

Killing the Bees

Honeybees pollinate one-third of all food crops and increase US crop values by $15 billion per year.[2] Since 2006, honeybees have suffered from colony collapse disorder, or CCD. In this disorder, worker bees disappear. They fail to return to the hive, leaving only the queen and some immature bees. The cause of CCD is unknown, but several factors are implicated: new diseases caused by viruses and fungi, new types of mites, lack of important nutrients due to fewer pollen and nectar sources, and especially pesticides called neonicotinoids. Less food is available when monocultures replace natural habitats. Insecticides intended to kill pest species also kill or weaken bees. Most experts think CCD occurs when several factors combine. The Environmental Protection Agency (EPA) announced in 2015 that it would withhold approval for the continued use of neonicotinoid pesticides until their effect on bees is better understood.

sustainable agriculture. "Change is no longer optional; it is a necessity," Ikerd said.[1]

In modern industrial agriculture, crops and animals are grown for food and sometimes, as in the case of cotton, for industrial use. These crops and animals are grown intensively, using modern technology and often using industrial processes. The main trait of sustainable agriculture is the ability to maintain a farm's productivity and profitability over the long term, while still benefiting society and the environment.

Sustainable and industrial agriculture are not mutually exclusive. Many industrial farmers use sustainable techniques such as efficient irrigation systems, crop rotation, or erosion control. Sustainable farmers use modern farm equipment, and some use "natural" pesticides produced by plants.

In general, the term *industrial farming* in this book will refer to intensive farming that does *not* involve sustainable methods. The term will include production that involves the use of monocultures, intensive irrigation, and synthetic fertilizers and pesticides. In the case of animals, the term will include factory farms.

Bees are important for pollinating plants.

Nonsustainable Cropping Systems

In the United States, crops such as corn, wheat, soybeans, cotton, and rice are typically grown in monocultures. Many farmers consider this an efficient way to grow large quantities of food or fiber quickly. But monocultures require huge inputs of chemicals, especially fertilizers and pesticides. Although a few natural ecosystems, such as wild rice, essentially grow as monocultures, growing the same crop year after year on the same field is unsustainable. Without crop variation—for example, by crop rotation—the plants deplete soil nutrients over time.

◢ What Is Global Warming?

Earth constantly receives heat energy from the sun. The planet absorbs some of this heat and reflects some back into the atmosphere. Gases called greenhouse gases (GHGs) trap the reflected heat and keep it in the atmosphere. The major GHGs are carbon dioxide, methane, and nitrous oxide. The trapping of heat, called the greenhouse effect, keeps Earth at a constant temperature and allows life to exist. Global warming is the gradual increase in Earth's average temperature due to the addition of excess GHGs to the atmosphere. Our current rapid temperature increase is primarily due to fossil fuel burning. The excess GHGs added by fossil fuels trap more heat, and Earth's temperature warms.

Industrial farmers replenish these nutrients by adding artificial fertilizers. Typical crops cannot withstand pest infestations, and without natural controls, harmful insects and weeds run rampant. Therefore, many farmers choose to control them with toxic pesticides. As a result, monocultures damage and pollute soils, kill organisms, and reduce habitat for birds, bees, and other organisms that would help sustain the system. Often, this starts a cycle that leads to the application of more and more synthetic fertilizers and pesticides.

A second feature of unsustainable agriculture, closely tied to monocultures, is the use of fossil fuels, or petroleum products made from coal, oil, or natural gas. While fueling farm machinery is the most obvious use, it is a small part of total fossil fuel use. Many fertilizers and pesticides are made of petroleum and are produced by industries that run on petroleum. Distributing the chemicals onto crops uses more fossil fuels, as does harvesting, packaging, processing, and transporting foods.

Using today's industrial farming methods, at least three calories of energy are needed to grow one calorie of vegetable food in the United States. Including the cost of processing and transportation, seven to ten calories are needed per calorie of food. Meat production is especially unsustainable;

production of one calorie of grain-fed beef requires 35 calories of energy.[3] While converting one form of energy—such as oil, sun, or wind—into food energy will always require an energy input, many processes in agriculture use much more energy than is sustainable in the long term.

In addition, the burning of fossil fuels causes serious damage to the environment and public health. Three byproducts of burning fossil fuel—carbon dioxide, methane, and nitrous oxide—are greenhouse gases and key contributors to global warming. Other byproducts contribute to the formation of acid rain and smog. These chemicals, along with particulate matter such as smoke and ash, increase respiratory and cardiac problems in humans.

Finally, industrial agriculture stresses water systems much more than sustainable agriculture does. Worldwide, agriculture consumes approximately 70 percent of the freshwater used, and 15 to 35 percent of this use is unsustainable. Farmers waste 60 percent of the water they use each year due to poor techniques, leaking irrigation systems, or cultivation of crops not suited to the local climate.[4]

Nonsustainable Animal Agriculture

Industrially raised large meat-producing animals, such as cattle and hogs, end their days in "finishing" facilities, where they are prepared for slaughter. These factory farms are called confined animal feeding operations (CAFOs). Animals in CAFOs are cramped together and fed a high-calorie grain diet to maximize weight gain.

Every year, US livestock and poultry operations together produce an estimated 500 million short tons (453 million metric tons) of manure—three times the amount produced by the human population. This untreated waste is stored in manure pits or lagoons, and ultimately, much of it is spread onto farm fields.

Stored manure emits noxious gases including ammonia and methane, which cause skin rashes, respiratory problems, headaches, and nervous system problems. Overcrowding in CAFOs causes diseases to spread. Constant use of antibiotic medicines in CAFO-raised animals causes bacteria to become resistant to the antibiotic. That is, every time the antibiotic is used, it becomes less effective at killing bacteria. This means either a higher dose or a different antibiotic must be used.

Transitioning to Sustainable Agriculture

Modern-day industrial agriculture is far from sustainable. Its huge production is based on monocultures and factory farms. This causes serious environmental problems including erosion of topsoil, water pollution, and water shortages. Industrial agriculture depends on fossil fuels, the use of which speeds up climate change. In addition, industrial agriculture's massive use of industrial chemicals poisons the environment and endangers human health.

◢ Pesticide Resistance

Just as bacteria develop antibiotic resistance, plants and animals develop resistance to pesticides. Application of a herbicide called glyphosate, marketed by Monsanto as Roundup, increased tenfold from 1996 to 2012. Monsanto also sells Roundup Ready crop seeds, which are designed to be resistant to glyphosate. Monsanto intended the herbicide to kill only the weeds, not the crop. But the weeds quickly developed herbicide resistance as well. Before 2000, no states reported glyphosate-resistant weeds. In 2012, 21 states reported glyphosate-resistant weeds, including 92 percent of Georgia farmers.[5]

Depending on the weed, the first application of herbicide may kill 83 to 98 percent of the weed population.[6] The most resistant weeds survive and produce the next generation. Thus, each generation becomes more resistant, and after only a few applications, a highly resistant strain—a "superweed"—results. Killing superweeds requires either a larger dose of the same herbicide or an entirely new herbicide. The same process occurs when insects become resistant to insecticides and develop into "superbugs."

Industrial feedlots often have thousands of animals in confined spaces.

The 1990 Farm Bill

The United States first addressed sustainable farming in the 1990 Farm Bill. The bill defined sustainable agriculture as "an integrated system of plant and animal production practices ... that will, over the long term:

» satisfy human food and fiber needs

» enhance environmental quality and the natural resource base upon which the agricultural economy depends

» make the most efficient use of nonrenewable resources and on-farm resources and integrate, where appropriate, natural biological cycles and controls

» sustain the economic viability of farm operations

» enhance the quality of life for farmers and society as a whole."[7]

In 1990, the US government passed a farm bill outlining goals for a more sustainable agricultural industry. Making the transition has not been easy or fast. But many farmers are now implementing new practices and technologies to help make this transition.

Sir Albert **Howard**
(1873–1947)

S ir Albert Howard was born in England, grew up on his family's rural estate, and studied botany at Cambridge University. During his 25 years abroad as a botanist, he directed agricultural centers and researched organic agriculture. His travels to places such as the West Indies and particularly India opened his eyes to different agricultural methods and made him a pioneer of the organic agriculture movement. Twenty-first century sustainable farmers continue to value his work.

One of Howard's best-known books is *An Agricultural Testament*, published in 1940, which describes natural farming techniques. It emphasizes growing mixed crops without artificial fertilizers and instead replenishing soil nutrients with compost. This technique was based on his observations in India, where farmers had developed composting to a high art. Howard also discovered that pests disappeared when the farmer corrected problems such as low soil fertility or growing a crop in an unsuitable location.

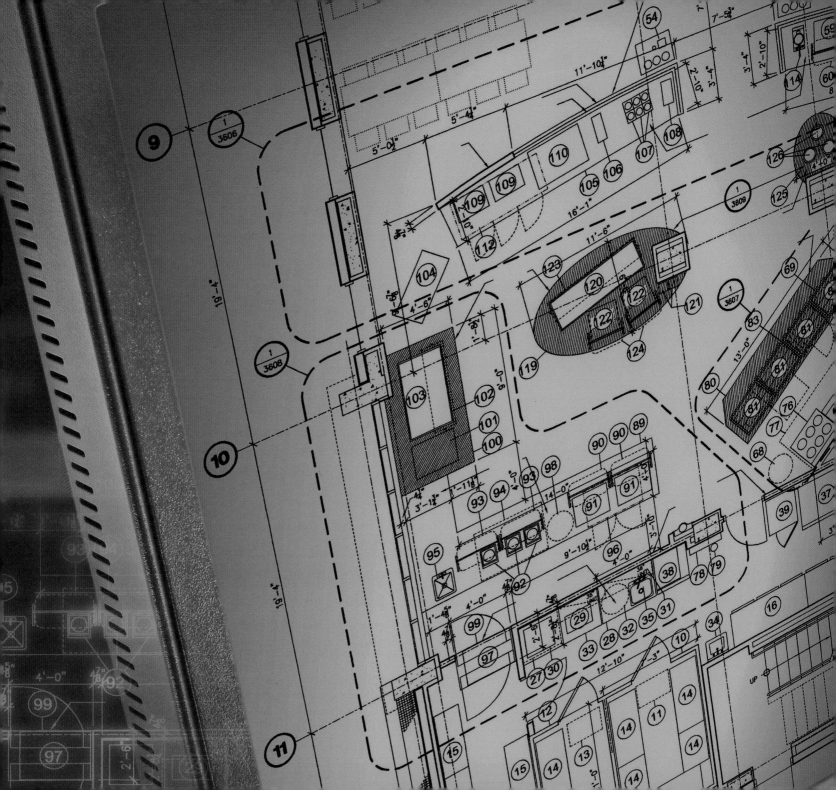

THREE

SUSTAINABLE SOIL

M ost secrets to sustainable soil are not new, and most involve techniques, not technology. Louis Sukovaty and Jennifer Argraves run the 150-acre (60 ha) Crown S Ranch in Winthrop, Washington.[1] After thoroughly researching sustainable agriculture, they concluded that some of the best techniques come from pre–World War II (1939–1945) research—a time before chemical fertilizers and pesticides. Sukovaty and Argraves use techniques designed to close nutrient cycles on their ranch; that is, they want to reach a point where the ranch can sustain itself without using synthetic fertilizers or pesticides.

To improve the soil, they use a seven-year rotation on each field. For example, a field may produce alfalfa during years one and two; the same field may be used for cattle during years three and four; year five may be for poultry, and years six and seven may be for grain. Sukovaty and Argraves use AutoCAD, a computerized design tool, to map the ranch and keep track of rotations. Portable electric fencing helps move

A software application called AutoCAD enables farmers to make detailed maps.

cattle and poultry around the fields within their years, so the animals do not constantly graze the same part of a field. Using this method, the farmers doubled the ranch's soil organic matter in the first ten years.

Compost is an important soil amendment that provides nutrients to plants and food for soil microbes.

The technique of raising several types of animals on the same land, which Argraves calls "layering," also benefits soil. It increases soil fertility because the manures have varying levels of nutrients and minerals. Different animals prefer different plants. Cows graze the tops of plants, while chickens clip plants near the ground and scratch the soil. Thus, rotation allows for more balanced grazing. Ultimately, this rotation-and-layering strategy produces more food per acre because each rotation adds different nutrients to the soil. The Crown S ranchers know healthy soil leads to high crop productivity. Thus, their key to sustainable farming is "Feed the soil, not the plant!"[2]

◢ What Is Soil?

Soil, the home of uncountable numbers of living organisms, consists of soil particles, air, water, and organic matter. All components must be present in the correct proportions to make healthy soil. Soil particles, which are classified based on their diameters, include sand (0.05 to 2 mm), silt (0.002 to 0.05 mm), and clay (smaller than 0.002 mm). The best soil for growing plants is loam, which is 7 to 27 percent clay, 28 to 50 percent silt, and up to 52 percent sand.[3] Sticky clay particles hold soil together and provide mineral nutrients. Sand particles allow water to drain through soil quickly. Silt provides texture and mineral nutrients. Pores, or small spaces, between sand and silt particles allow air and water circulation. A small percentage of loam, as of all soils, is organic matter—decayed plant and animal parts that also provide nutrients for plant growth. Most organic matter is in the topsoil.

Soil Organic Matter

Soil carries out four functions necessary for plant growth. It holds the plant's roots in place, supplies the plant with water, supplies air to the roots, and provides mineral nutrients. Living organisms are essential to all

these functions. Most soil organisms are in the topsoil. A single teaspoon of healthy topsoil contains more living organisms than there are people on Earth.

In general, high levels of topsoil organic matter are essential for healthy, productive, and sustainable soil. Yet many farmers fail to replenish organic matter, or they allow it to degrade through erosion or over-tilling. But not all organic matter is the same. Different additives and soil organisms have varying effects on soil health.

For sustainable farmers, the most important source of organic matter is crop residue left to decay into the soil. Another important source is referred to as green manure. This may include cover crops grown after cash crops are harvested, or intercropped species grown at the same time. Other sources are animal manure, biosolids (sewage sludge), or processing wastes from industries such as vegetable processing plants or breweries. Too much organic matter added from outside sources, such as animal manure or biosolids, may harm plants or run off and cause water pollution. The EPA requires treatment and testing of biosolids in the sewage treatment plant, so they are low-risk additives if added in proper amounts.

When choosing organic matter, one important factor is the ratio of the mass of carbon to the mass of nitrogen in the substance. This is also known as the C:N ratio. Carbon provides energy and materials for organisms to make organic compounds. Nitrogen is required for them to make proteins. Organisms obtain both carbon and nitrogen from the plant or animal food they eat. Each type of organism has its own C:N ratio, and the organism must eat food that supplies the needed amounts of carbon and nitrogen. An ideal C:N ratio for soil organic matter, which feeds plants and soil organisms, is approximately 24:1.[4] "Brown" materials such as sawdust and straw are high in carbon, while "green" materials such as manure, alfalfa, and compost are high in nitrogen and promote fast growth.

◂ C:N Ratios

The C:N ratio is important when planning cover crops or crop rotations or when making compost. Soil microbes must eat to maintain their C:N ratio of approximately 8:1. They lose carbon during respiration, so they must consume food with a much higher C:N ratio—specifically, a ratio of 24:1, of which 16 parts of carbon are used in respiration and 8 are used for maintenance. Thus, a C:N ratio of 24:1 is ideal for compost or soil organic matter. Mature alfalfa hay has an almost perfect ratio of 25:1. A higher C:N ratio, such as straw at 80:1, slows the rate of decomposition. A lower ratio, such as cattle manure at 17:1, speeds it up.[7]

Soil organic matter builds up soil, improving its texture and making it more fertile for future years. It also provides nutrients for the current year's crop, reducing the need for other fertilizers. During the first year, roughly half of freshly applied residue or manure will be broken down by microbes and become available for plants to use. Smaller amounts will be available in succeeding years. Soil organic matter should be added every year to keep soil healthy.

Soil Erosion

Soil erosion occurs when wind or water removes topsoil faster than it can be replaced. Only 0.4 inches (1 cm) of soil forms every 100 to 400 years, so it can take 3,000 to 12,000 years to build enough soil to grow crops.[5] Because soil is replenished so slowly, it is considered a nonrenewable resource. Many common industrial farming practices cause soil erosion. These include keeping too many animals on the land, allowing animals to overgraze, plowing land to produce annual crops, and failing to rotate crops.

According to the World Wildlife Fund, an environmental organization, half of Earth's topsoil has been lost in the past 150 years.[6] Ultimately, erosion does not just degrade soil; it turns land into desert. Erosion has also increased water pollution, causing declines in fish and other aquatic species. In addition, soil health suffers from compaction, loss of structure, loss of nutrients, and increasing

concentrations of salt due to irrigation. Compaction refers to pressing soil particles together; this reduces soil pores and disrupts air and water circulation. Wheel traffic from farm equipment is the major cause, but lack of crop rotation also contributes. Rotating crops prevents compaction by allowing different types of root systems to penetrate and break up the soil. Overall, land has become less arable, and its ability to retain water has decreased, which increases flooding.

No-Till Plus Cover Crops

According to the USDA, "Tilling the soil is the equivalent of an earthquake, hurricane, tornado, and forest fire occurring simultaneously to the world of soil organisms."[8] Tilling destroys soil structure and soil organism habitat. The standard sustainable method used for treating these problems is conservation tillage, which leaves at least 30 percent of the ground covered with crop residue after planting. No-till methods leave 50 to 100 percent of the residue in place.[9] These methods drastically reduce soil erosion. They also reduce sediment and air pollution because much less soil enters the water and air. No-till methods increase organism activity in all soils, and they increase carbon levels in the top layers of most soils. In addition, these methods reduce fossil fuel use and soil compaction because farmers use less equipment.

Keeping the soil covered year-round also improves soil health. The sugars that plants make during photosynthesis are soil organisms' best food. Thus, the area surrounding plant roots is these organisms' banquet table. Plants and microbes exchange food. Plants release some of their sugars into the soil surrounding the roots. Microbes feed on these sugars and release nutrients that plants can absorb and use. As aboveground crop residue and roots decay, they add to soil organic matter.

No-till farming is sustainable in the sense that it adds to soil organic matter and decreases erosion, compacting, and fossil fuel use—but it is unsustainable in one important way. Most farmers combine no-till with the use of pesticides to control weeds, and they plant new crops through the killed crop residue. This process negates many of the benefits of sustainability.

Organic farmers maintain no-till systems by using cover crops, which provide food for plants and soil organisms, suppress weed growth, prevent erosion, and store water. Before planting the cash crop, they use a new machine called the roller-crimper, developed by the Rodale Institute, a major organic research organization. This tool rolls over the cover crop, crushing and compressing the stems and turning them into mulch. The roller-crimper mounts on the front of the tractor, and a no-till seed drill mounts on the back, so crimping and planting are done in one pass. Going over the field only once saves fuel and compacts the soil less. A no-till drill controls the depth at which seeds are planted and the rate seeds are dropped. A blade slices open the soil, seed is fed out through a tube, and a structure called a press wheel covers the seed with soil. Seeding is done through the cover crop, which barely disturbs the soil compared to typical tilling and planting. The roller-crimper is still being tested, but it shows promising results. Its use could eliminate the use of herbicides and make no-till farming truly sustainable.

Plant Biodiversity

Plant diversity improves soil health in ways monocultures cannot. Biodiversity creates different habitats that stimulate activity of different soil organisms, and it adds soil nutrients. One way to create biodiversity is by crop rotation, or alternating the crops planted in the same field—for example, planting corn one year and soybeans the next year.

A farmer practices intercropping, planting rubber trees and pineapples in the same field.

Another way is intercropping, or planting two or more crops in the same field at the same time. In the United States, intercropping usually happens on small, organic farms, not on large-scale industrial farms. Crops are planted in alternating strips, with each managed separately. Intercropping increases crop yield. It can also improve pest control, water and soil conservation, and the movement of nutrients through soil and organisms. But these advantages depend on proper management, level of environmental stresses, and finding crops that work well together.

33

Synthetic Soil

In nature, soil breathes: its microbes reproduce, transform soil, die, and return to the soil. But urban soil systems are unsustainable. Living soil covered with concrete cannot breathe. Nutrients are not recycled; people remove garbage to landfills, where it only partially decomposes and never returns.

Dr. Rachel Armstrong, a British architect, hopes to extend sustainable soils to cities as well as agriculture. "Soils are a form of technology," Armstrong says.

"They perform useful work transforming one group of substances into another."[10]

To bring sustainable agriculture technologies to cities, Armstrong combines inorganic, or nonliving, chemical structures with gels to produce soil-like formations. She wants to extend these soil-like ecosystems to unused spaces within cities, such as cavities in building walls. Her artificial soils may someday help heat buildings, filter water, collect toxins, and insulate living spaces.

The USDA recommends we view the soil as a living factory that works for us, and treat it properly to keep it working well. This includes feeding it constantly with organic matter and managing it to be as productive as possible, without destroying it in the process. These techniques require little technology but great understanding of the soil ecosystem.

The Rodale **Family**

In North America, the phrase *organic gardening* is most associated with the Rodale family. J. I. Rodale (1898–1971) founded the Rodale Institute in 1947 to promote links between healthy soil, food, and people. On his Pennsylvania farm, Rodale experimented with organic farming methods, while the rest of the country embraced chemical fertilizers.

When J. I. Rodale died in 1971, his son Robert took over the business. Robert and his wife, Ardath, developed a 333-acre (135 ha) research farm to test organic methods. Testimony by Robert and other organic proponents convinced the US Congress to include funds for organic agriculture in the 1985 Farm Bill. In the 2000s, Robert and Ardath's children, Anthony and Maria, have served as chairs of the Rodale Institute's board of directors. The institute's research, educational, and community outreach programs continue to expand.

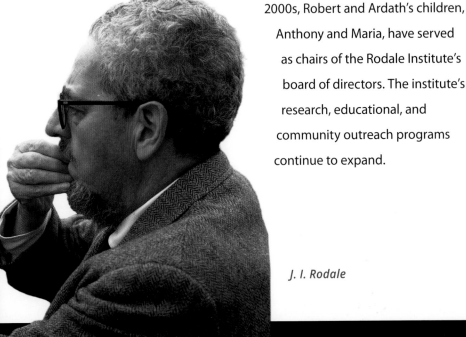

J. I. Rodale

How Organic Matter Changes

Soil organic matter is required to grow plants. But organic matter does not stay the same. It constantly changes due to processes in the soil. These include:

1. **Additions:** When roots and leaves die, they become part of soil organic matter. Dead animal bodies and waste products also add to organic matter.

2. **Breakdown and waste:** Soil organisms break down plant and animal residue into a series of compounds. Soil organisms reproduce and release wastes into the soil.

3. **Formation of plant food:** Waste products of soil organisms and breakdown products of organic matter become plant nutrients.

4. **Stabilization:** When soil organic matter breaks down completely, it resists further changes and stabilizes. New organic matter is added continually and goes through the above changes.

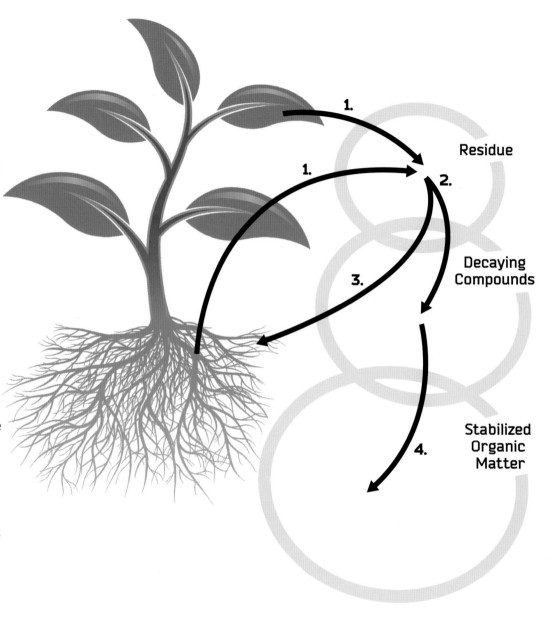

1.

1.

Residue

2.

3.

Decaying Compounds

4.

Stabilized Organic Matter

FOUR

CHEMICALS AND PRECISION AGRICULTURE

Crops quickly deplete soil nutrients and attract both weed and insect pests. This has led to an explosion of agricultural chemical use since the 1940s—synthetic fertilizers to replace nutrients and synthetic pesticides to destroy pests. Both are unsustainable and have caused serious environmental and public health impacts. However, before pesticides were used, farmers lost significant amounts of crops to insects, weeds, and diseases. This too was unsustainable. Sustainable agriculture researchers are looking for ways to maintain or increase crop production while decreasing the use of both fertilizers and pesticides.

Insects such as caterpillars can destroy a farmer's crops.

Precision Agriculture

A farmer checks his GPS from inside his tractor.

Adding excess nitrogen fertilizer to crops wastes money, increases fertilizer runoff that pollutes waterways, and releases greenhouse gases into the atmosphere. Farmers try to use nitrogen efficiently by applying appropriate levels of fertilizer—no more or less than they need. The techniques they use to accomplish this are called precision agriculture.

First, farmers make many measurements of soil or leaf nitrogen to show the pattern of nutrient content throughout a field. Global positioning systems (GPS) receive satellite information, and geographic information system (GIS) software manages data collected by remote sensing tools to show how the crop is growing in each section of the field. This technology helps farmers view their fields as many small, individual sections rather than as large, single units. Farmers can tailor the application of seed, water, fertilizer, or pesticides to each specific section, using only the precise amounts needed. This method makes farming more efficient and uses less energy. Future farmers might even sit in offices and direct tractors fitted with auto-steering mechanisms and GPS. However, equipment is expensive, so precision farming is not necessarily cheaper.

Precision agriculture also decreases soil compaction and fossil fuel use because the tractor runs over only the parts of the field that need fertilizer or other additions. More of the field remains untouched. Precision agriculture technologies are currently associated with conventional industrial farming, but they are valuable because they make conventional farming more sustainable. These technologies can also be applied to sustainable operations.

Nanotechnology in Agriculture

As fossil fuel resources decline and industrial agriculture becomes increasingly inadequate, researchers are looking for new technologies to maintain high levels of food production. Nanotechnology is one possibility. In nanotechnology, very tiny particles—atoms, molecules, or clusters of molecules—are either manipulated or assemble themselves to make new structures with specific characteristics. These new structures range in size from 0.1 to 100 nanometers.[1] One nanometer is one billionth of a meter. A piece of paper is approximately 100,000 nanometers thick.

Some nanotechnology structures are natural substances. Some can improve soil fertility by slowly releasing nitrogen and phosphorus into the soil or making soil micronutrients more available to plants. Others might remove toxic substances or improve the soil's ability to retain water. They use natural chemical processes such as ion exchange, in which charged particles on the nanostructures replace charged particles in the soil. Another process involves attaching and detaching nutrient particles from water molecules. Other nanotechnology structures are GPS-linked electronic sensors. They would be placed throughout fields to monitor crop growth and soil nutrient content, making precision agriculture even more precise. Many possible nanotechnology applications are being studied.

Research on uses of nanotechnology in agriculture has increased since 2010, but it is still a tiny part of agricultural research and is growing slowly. Nanotechnology could go in many directions, and care is needed to ensure it is used sustainably.

Pesticides and Integrated Pest Management

Pesticides are one of the least sustainable aspects of modern industrial agriculture. In the 1940s, they were considered magic bullets that could eliminate crop pests and increase yields. Regulation was

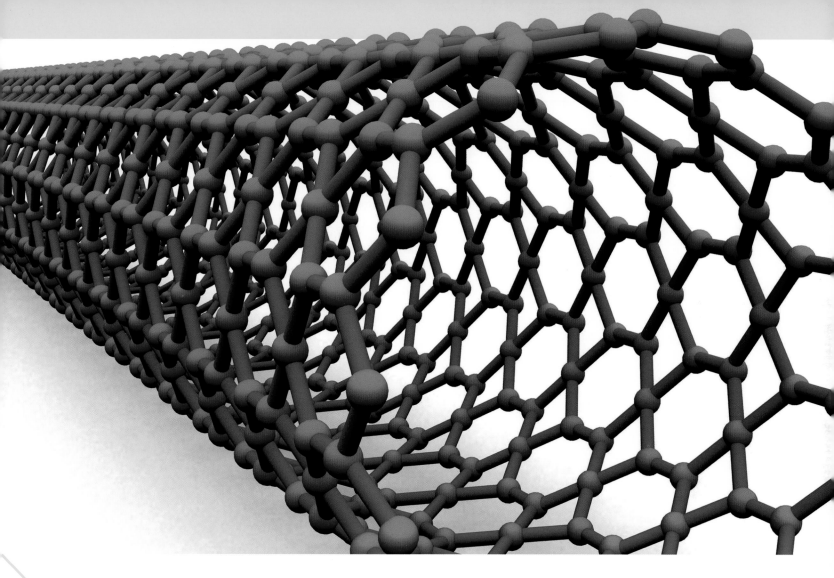

Research has shown that tiny carbon tubes known as nanotubes can help plants grow. Further studies are needed to determine whether they are safe.

minimal. Not until the 1960s, after publication of scientist and author Rachel Carson's book *Silent Spring*, did the public or the federal government seriously consider the possible health or environmental effects of pesticides. The government tightened regulations in 1972 and has done so several times since.

The EPA and USDA support the use of integrated pest management (IPM) to decrease pesticide use. IPM is the control of agricultural pests using a combination of methods designed to cause the least possible damage to people, property, and the environment. It relies on information about pest life cycles and interactions with the environment. It recommends that pesticides be used as a last resort. But IPM first strives to prevent pest problems without pesticides—for example, by using crop rotation, choosing pest-resistant seed varieties, and ensuring roots are pest-free before planting.

When pest control is needed, IPM recommends using the least risky control methods first. These include mechanical controls such as mowing, weeding, or trapping insects; targeted nontoxic chemicals that disrupt insect mating; or beneficial insects, which are predators or parasites of the pests. Insecticides are used last, starting with targeted spraying. Farmers spray the entire field only as a last resort.

Pesticides by the Numbers

The US government introduced sustainable agriculture in the 1990 Farm Bill. However, this has not decreased pesticide use. EPA data from 2007 show a slight decline from 948 million pounds (430 million kg) to 877 million pounds (398 million kg) between 2000 and 2007. But use of the herbicide glyphosate has skyrocketed, from 85 million pounds (39 million kg) in 2001 to 180 million pounds (82 million kg) in 2007.[2] By 2012, glyphosate usage had reached 280 million pounds (127 million kg).[3]

Making Pest Control More Sustainable

Most farmers take a reactive approach to IPM. They interpret IPM to mean simply monitoring fields and scheduling the best time to apply pesticides. They act only after pests are sighted; they ignore the biological or preventive approach, which was the original goal of IPM. A much more sustainable approach is biointensive IPM, which emphasizes proactive

Rachel Carson
(1907–1964)

Rachel Carson grew up in Springdale, Pennsylvania, a rural river town. She absorbed a lifelong love of nature from her mother. Carson attended Pennsylvania College for Women, now known as Chatham College, and studied at the Woods Hole Marine Biological Laboratory. She received a master's degree in zoology from Johns Hopkins University. Carson was a marine biologist and a science editor for the US Fish and Wildlife Service. She wrote several best-selling books on sea life, but her 1962 book *Silent Spring* made her a monumental voice in the sustainable agriculture movement. The book sparked an environmental movement and a worldwide discussion of the dangers of pesticide use.

Throughout the 1950s, aggressive spraying of the pesticide DDT to control mosquitoes wiped out many bird populations. This alerted Carson to pesticide dangers. She compiled evidence on the effects of indiscriminate pesticide use and warned of "silent springs" without songbirds. After publishing *Silent Spring*, Carson persevered despite attacks from the chemical industry and government officials. In 1963, testifying before a Senate subcommittee, she said, "Our heedless and destructive acts enter into the vast cycles of the earth and in time return to bring hazard to ourselves."[4]

measures. Biointensive IPM has characteristics of reactive IPM, such as monitoring, planning, and using pest-resistant varieties. However, farmers using biointensive IPM must also understand the biology and ecology of beneficial and pest organisms. They must design the crop system so the pest organism has a disadvantage and its parasites and predators have an advantage. They maintain a healthy, biodiverse ecosystem both above and below ground to create habitat for beneficial organisms. This results in less, or no, need for pesticides. An excellent example of a proactive IPM system is the Washington State tree fruit industry's use of the WSU Decision Aid System (DAS). This computer modeling system uses models of pest biology and weather data to help farmers monitor and manage pests in their location based on specific field conditions.

Biotechnology also has the potential to make pest control more sustainable. But like IPM, it is often used in unsustainable ways. Biotechnology is any technology that changes biological processes. In agriculture, it usually refers to the use of genetic modification (GM), also called genetic engineering. GM changes the genetic makeup of an organism by adding or removing genes. A prominent example is Roundup Ready corn and soybeans, designed to be resistant to the herbicide Roundup. The Roundup Ready crop grows, the farmer sprays Roundup, and Roundup kills weeds but not the crop.

Unfortunately, the chemical company was so eager to get Roundup Ready technology on the market and make a profit that it released the technology prematurely. This has led to Roundup Ready crops being unsustainable. First, weeds quickly become resistant to the herbicide, so higher herbicide concentrations or stronger herbicides must be used. This process increases rather than decreases pesticide use, because resistant superweeds are harder to kill. Second, the increase in pesticides leads to an increase in fossil fuel use, since fossil fuels are needed for both making and applying the herbicide. Third, Roundup is highly toxic, and the World Health Organization (WHO) has indicated it is

How Genetic Modification Works

Genetic modification changes the genetic makeup of cells, forming a new organism with new characteristics. This can involve transferring DNA from one species to another, transferring DNA within a species, or "knockout" technology in which genes are turned off or made inoperative. Each gene directs an organism to make a specific protein. When an organism receives a new gene, it makes a new protein. Similar to selective breeding, in which people grow plants specifically to produce desired traits, genetic modification results in new traits. With genetic modification, however, the process occurs with greater speed and efficiency. In selective breeding, parents must be closely related. In genetic modification, a gene can be transferred from any species with the desired trait. Examples of genetically engineered crop plants include pesticide-resistant plants; golden rice, which produces higher levels of vitamin A; and longer-lasting tomatoes.

probably cancer-causing. Experts believe Roundup Ready could have been effective for decades, and perhaps even centuries, if the chemical company had waited for additional technology development.

A potentially more sustainable example of GM use is the production of plant-incorporated protectants, or PIPs. To make a PIP, scientists might locate a plant producing a chemical that kills or repels a certain insect. They copy the gene that makes this chemical and, using GM, insert it into a crop plant. The crop plant then makes the natural pesticide. In this way, the crop is protected without using toxic synthetic pesticides. However, some experts fear that, if not properly implemented, PIP technology may suffer from the same problems as Roundup Ready technology.

Best Practices for Sustainable Pest Control

Many alternatives to pesticides exist. One is plant breeding. Many crop varieties have been bred that are resistant to specific pests and diseases. Some wheat varieties, for example, are resistant to stem rust,

Reporters observe dead insects on a Roundup Ready soybean plant.

leaf rust, powdery mildew, Hessian fly, and others. While useful, resistant varieties can lose their resistance, and new pests can emerge. Thus, other techniques are needed.

A second alternative is biological control, or the introduction of predators or parasites that feed on insect pests. This method is most effective for perennial crops, where fields are seldom disturbed and control organisms can become established. Annual crops may require multiple releases of predator organisms, but this is expensive and used only for high-value fruit and vegetable crops. One success story is the protection of cassava in Africa. Cassava is a starchy root that is an important tropical crop. A parasite introduced by farmers now effectively controls the mealy bug that attacks cassava. In other cases, ecologists recommend improving habitat for native natural enemies rather than introducing new species. The farmer can plant patches of predator habitat within the field or along the edges, or plant several crops in the same field. Experts say the most successful approach is likely a combination of habitat development and the introduction of beneficial organisms.

The techniques used to improve soil and crops also help control pests and disease organisms. These techniques include improving soil organic matter, improving fertility, choosing appropriate irrigation methods, and implementing crop rotation. Although these methods are effective, they require significant understanding of pest biology and the ecology of the crop system. Methods exist to greatly reduce the use of chemicals, both fertilizers and pesticides, in agriculture. However, using chemicals is easier. Chemicals often give farmers the exact results they want, whereas biological approaches are more complex and give mixed results—especially when farmers lack training in their use. Many farmers adopt sustainable methods only when they are consistently successful, such as insect mating disruption. Chemical companies are motivated to sell products, and until recently have been only marginally motivated by sustainable methods. But many have begun to adopt a new approach.

◂ Natural Pest Management

Environmentally sound pest control works with nature. Cotton farms along China's Yangtze River are plagued with cotton-destroying boll weevils. A Chinese professor identified more than 100 species of spiders that prey on the boll weevil. He showed farmers how to attract spiders to their fields by digging small holes in the fields and providing grass cover for hiding places. Spiders have decreased pesticide use by 80 percent and increased farmers' cotton yields.[5]

At Avondale Wines in South Africa, 100 ducks patrol 247 acres (100 ha) of vineyards.[6] The ducks happily eat snails, leaving the rest of the vineyard intact. Snails love grapes, so the ducks are removing a major pest, and wine growers no longer need toxic pesticides.

Rather than simply trying to sell their product, companies are starting to look at their relationships with farmers as a long-term partnership—and profitable farmers are better long-term customers.

Some farmers use ducks as natural pest control. The ducks eat bugs that would otherwise damage crops.

FIVE

SEEDS AND BIOTECHNOLOGY

Mas Masumoto grew up on a small peach farm in California's Central Valley. After college, he returned with his new wife, Marcy, to run the farm. But by 1987, buyers no longer wanted his peaches. The peach variety, known as Suncrest, "tasted great, like a peach is supposed to," Masumoto said, but "it was an old heirloom variety that didn't have the right cosmetics for the marketplace."[1] Masumoto hired a bulldozer to destroy his peach orchard. He also wrote an essay, "Epitaph for a Peach," which was published in the *Los Angeles Times*. People who read his essay began writing him letters saying, "Keep this peach!" He canceled the bulldozer. Mas became an organic farmer and made contacts with farmers' markets and restaurants where people valued the peach's flavor over its appearance. The peach farm became a landmark in the local food movement.

Mas Masumoto picks a peach off a tree at his farm in California.

The Decline of Seeds

The temperature inside the Svalbard Global Seed Vault is 0°F (–18°C).

Masumoto's experience is only one example of the difficulties sustainable farmers deal with in the face of industrial agriculture. Old crop varieties are dying out, often due to diseases, and there is little to replace them. An analysis of plant and animal breeding indicates budget cuts eliminated more than one-third of US plant-breeding programs between 1994 and 2014. Public and university plant breeders are disappearing. In the 1960s, there were 25 public corn breeders; in 2014, there were five.[2] Farmers have fewer seed choices, and lower farm biodiversity leaves their crops more vulnerable to diseases and pests.

In 1996, three giant companies controlled 22 percent of the global seed market. In 2014, they controlled more than half.[3] These companies concentrate their efforts on high-profit, high-acreage crops such as soybeans. They neglect other crops, including small grains, fruits, vegetables, organic crops, cover crops, and regional varieties. They file patents to restrict use of their seeds. Farmers are forbidden to save or share seeds, and other companies are forbidden to improve them, further restricting farmers' seed choices. Lack of staff and money

Svalbard Global Seed Vault

Around the world, more than 1,700 gene banks hold collections of food crop seeds. But these locations are vulnerable to factors such as war, climate change, natural disasters, lack of funding, and poor management. The Svalbard Global Seed Vault stores backups, or duplicates, of seeds from all of the world's storage facilities. It is located on an island in the Svalbard archipelago, halfway between mainland Norway and the North Pole. The seeds, located underground beneath permanently frozen soil and deep rock, remain dry and frozen even without power, and they are safe from disasters and climate changes. The vault can store 4.5 million crop varieties, or 2.5 billion seeds. As of 2015, it contained approximately 860,000 seed samples, including seeds from every country in the world.[4] It is the world's largest, most secure site for the storing of Earth's plant genetic diversity.

threaten public seed collections in the United States. People caring for these collections must choose which seeds to keep up to date and ready for planting. The rest are lost, depleting the country's genetic seed diversity and decreasing the ability to respond to future challenges.

Teff, a crop native to Ethiopia, is high in protein and calcium.

Food security is a worldwide problem, and nations are considering how to improve the world seed supply. The Gaia Foundation, a British charity that works on world sustainability problems, is leading a campaign to promote seed diversity and food security. The organization is increasingly concerned about the threat to biodiversity posed by commercial hybrid and GM seeds. Many native crops, such as the Ethiopian grain teff, are extremely nutritious. Farmers throughout Africa and Asia save seeds and replant them the next year. But if they buy GM seeds, or even if their harvest is contaminated by drifting GM pollen, they are forbidden to save the seeds. When large corporations control seeds around the globe, farmers lose the biodiversity of their native plants, the variety in their diets, and often their livelihoods.

Are GM Seeds Sustainable?

Some experts and farmers consider the use of biotechnology, particularly GM seeds, essential to combating global challenges such as climate change and population growth. They say GM crops allow production of more food on less land, and they ease environmental problems by decreasing herbicide use and soil erosion. The Biotechnology Industry Organization states that, in 2007, use of GM crops removed 31.2 billion pounds (14 billion kg) of carbon dioxide from the atmosphere, which is approximately equal to removing 6.3 million cars from the road.[5] The organization Food Insight points out that bioengineered crops, in addition to improving crop yields and increasing the nutritional quality of foods, are also more likely to resist droughts and other climate changes.

In the United States, more than half of all corn, soybeans, and cotton are now GM crops. The most common GM plants produce their own insecticides or resist herbicides. According to the National Academies, when seeds are grown as directed, "GM crops have been effective at reducing pest problems with economic and environmental benefits to farmers."[6] The organization cites improvements in soil and water quality, and reduced exposure of farm workers to pesticides. The group also describes the potential for GM crops to address food insecurity and climate change but says these benefits have yet to be demonstrated.

The Barilla Center for Food and Nutrition is an Italian organization that analyzes scientific, social, and political issues related to food and nutrition. According to the Barilla Center, genetically modified organisms (GMOs) "do not seem to play a significant role in alleviating hunger in the world for one simple reason: they were not developed with this goal in mind."[7] The Barilla Center does not see GMOs as a potential solution to environmental problems or natural resource depletion. They say GMOs have been in the environment for too short a time to produce clear-cut evidence, and their environmental effects are difficult to study. The only definitive data available are for herbicide resistance, which negatively affects

◢ Seed Savers Exchange

Various organizations work to save heirloom fruit and vegetable seeds to preserve Earth's plant genetic heritage and provide an alternative to "big agriculture." One of the largest in the United States is the Seed Savers Exchange (SSE) in Decorah, Iowa. It maintains thousands of plant varieties, grows and stores seeds, and documents cultural information and histories on their varieties. Farmers and gardeners donate seeds and their seeds' stories. SSE also produces a catalog through which they distribute heirloom varieties to members and the public. Their online resources give information on how to grow and preserve the seeds of many plants. SSE stores their varieties in Iowa and in two backup locations: the USDA Seed Bank in Fort Collins, Colorado, and Svalbard Global Seed Vault in Norway.

sustainability because it stimulates herbicide use, leading to a more toxic environment and more fossil fuel use. Other studies indicate, but do not prove, possible risks associated with GMO crops, including loss of biodiversity and damage to native habitats. Overall, because GMO crops are so new, it is too early to be certain of their effects, either positive or negative.

Making Seed Production Sustainable

The National Sustainable Agriculture Coalition (NSAC) emphasizes the need to revitalize public seed supplies and get more types of seeds to farmers. The organization has several recommendations for doing this. First, it recommends a comprehensive national plan to expand the number of plant breeders, particularly by restoring funding and supporting breeding programs at universities. Second, it suggests rewarding farmers for biodiversity measures, which provide farmers with greater seed choice. Third, the group encourages farmers to save and share seeds, and to promote regional seed companies, to counteract the current trend toward seed ownership by a few giant companies. Fourth, the coalition calls for funding to upgrade seed storage facilities and to improve sharing of this resource both nationally and internationally. Finally, it wants to educate the public and policymakers about the importance of plant breeding and its links to food availability and climate change. Of course, healthy soil is important to sustainable agriculture, but without healthy seeds, there is no agriculture.

Two opposing trends in this area are the rapid rate at which GM seeds are engulfing the market, and attempts by smaller farmers and gardeners to preserve remaining heritage seeds. Because diverse seed types are necessary for sustainability, farmers might best ensure seed sustainability, as NSAC recommends, by concentrating more on heritage seeds and less on GM seeds. GM seeds of the right type—those designed to resist drought, increase levels of important nutrients, or produce their own natural pesticides—could be highly sustainable. But most GM seeds in the mid-2010s are

herbicide-resistant seeds, which may have environmental consequences. As long as only a few companies control GM seeds, they are unlikely to make agriculture more sustainable or help solve twenty-first century problems.

At the Seed Savers Exchange, plants are grown in test tubes to protect them from viruses and bacteria.

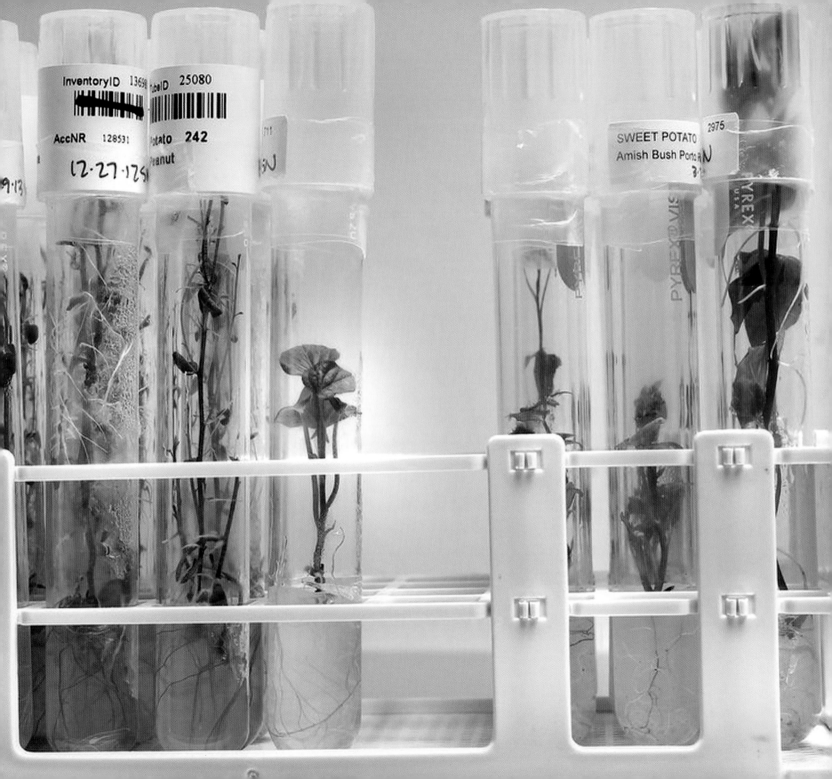

PERMACULTURE

The word *permaculture*, coined in the 1970s by Australians Bill Mollison and Dave Holmgren, is a combination of the words *permanent* and *agriculture*. It describes a sustainable agricultural system consisting of perennial or self-perpetuating plants. Permaculture systems mimic nature while still producing food, fiber, and energy for humans.

Dr. Wes Jackson, a plant geneticist, has spent his career trying to develop a permaculture replacement for modern monocultures. In 1976, Jackson turned his Salina, Kansas, farm into a nonprofit organization called The Land Institute. He recruited young plant breeders with PhDs for a long-term project designed to solve "the 10,000-year-old problem of agriculture." Jackson understood that replanting food crops such as corn and wheat annually required plowing and chemical use that caused devastating soil, nutrient, and energy loss. "The solution," he decided, "is to build an agriculture based on the way nature's ecosystems work." He looked to his native Kansas prairie.[8]

For four decades, Jackson and his plant breeders have crossbred wheat and other grains with perennial prairie grasses. One of their successes is the grain Kernza. Kernza is similar to wheat—but because it is a perennial, farmers do not have to plant new seeds every year. In addition, the plant's large root system holds the soil in place, helping to prevent erosion. Kernza is already on the menu in some places. Birchwood Café in Minneapolis, Minnesota, uses pancake mix containing Kernza; WheatFields, a bakery in Lawrence, Kansas, uses it to make bread; and Lawrence's Free State Brewery has used it in beer. While a long way from replacing crop monocultures, Jackson's permaculture research is making progress.

Edible landscaping is the practice of growing food alongside decorative plants.

SIX

SUSTAINABLE
WATER

Every year, the state of California conducts a spring snow survey at selected locations in the Sierra Nevada Mountains. The survey helps officials predict the amount of snowmelt that will enter reservoirs and be available to meet that year's water needs. On April 1, 2015, the amount of snow present was only 5 percent of the amount normally seen on that day—the lowest since recordkeeping began in 1950.[1] Speaking from one survey site, Governor Jerry Brown said, "Today we are standing on dry grass where there should be five feet of snow. This historic drought demands unprecedented action."[2] The governor then announced an executive order requiring a 25 percent reduction in water use by cities and towns across the state. It was California's first-ever mandatory water use reduction.

Mountains in the Sierra Nevada range were nearly snowless in April 2015.

A Water Crisis

Water-pumping windmills tap into the Ogallala Aquifer.

In 2015, California was in its fourth year of record drought, which was the worst since 1895. California agriculture depends on snowmelt for much of its water supply, and it uses a huge amount of water. The state's Central Valley, 450 miles (720 km) long and up to 60 miles (100 km) wide, supplies most of the country's vegetables. Eighty-five percent of the United States' carrots, plus most of the country's tomatoes, lettuce, asparagus, broccoli, melons, almonds, and grapes, come from this region.[3] All of it relies on irrigation.

California's long-standing drought worsened an already serious water problem. Most freshwater is stored as groundwater in spongelike aquifers deep underground. Groundwater, similar to oil, has been there for thousands or millions of years. Rain, snow, and streamflow normally refill aquifers. But as water needs grow and the drought progresses, people pump more water from the aquifers. This lowers the water table, or the depth underground at which water can be found. In 2015, groundwater supplied almost 60 percent of California's water needs, and wells that once struck water at 500 feet (150 m) had to be drilled to 1,000 feet (300 m) or more.[4]

California is not alone. Between 2004 and 2013, the Colorado River Basin lost 15.6 cubic miles (65 cu km) of water, and three-fourths of the loss was groundwater. This is twice the water capacity of Lake Mead, the country's largest reservoir. The Ogallala Aquifer, which runs through the Midwest from South Dakota into Texas, is losing groundwater at unprecedented rates due to deep irrigation wells supplying thirsty crops such as corn and alfalfa. Between 2004 and 2013, the water table in the Texas panhandle fell 15 feet (5 m). A study from Kansas State University calculated the Ogallala Aquifer will decline by 69 percent by the 2060s.[5] Due to climate change, droughts are expected to worsen in

the coming decades. Dry regions, such as the American Southwest, will likely expand and suffer long droughts followed by extreme precipitation events, including flooding.

Agriculture and Water

In the United States, agriculture accounts for 80 percent of all freshwater used each year.[6] Sixteen percent of US cropland is irrigated, but because most of this land is used to grow high-value crops, it represents nearly half of crop sales.[7] California and the Colorado River basin, which have the most severe water shortages, also have the most rapid population growth. California's population was 38.8 million in 2014 and is projected to reach 60 million by 2050.[8] The most growth will be seen in urban southern California, where water is already scarce.

According to a 2012 Department of the Interior study, water demand in the Colorado River basin will exceed supply by more than 1 trillion gallons (3.8 trillion L) by 2060; for comparison, a single household typically uses 325,000 gallons (1.2 million L) of water per year.[9] Meanwhile, population growth will increase stress on already limited water supplies. This will increase water prices, leading to hikes in both irrigation costs and food prices.

The USDA estimates increasing irrigation efficiency by only 10 percent could save the United States $200 million per year in fuel costs alone. Animal agriculture could also benefit from efficiency measures. Dairy farmers who clean their cattle houses using automatic systems that release the same amount of water each time use 150 gallons (568 L) of water per cow per day; those who use only the amount of water needed use only five to ten gallons (19 to 38 L) per cow per day.[10] Industrial farms also release pollutants that overfertilize and contaminate water supplies. These include disease-causing microbes, antibiotics, hormones, heavy metals, salts, solid organic matter, and nutrients such as ammonia and

nitrates from fertilizer and manure. The pollutants enter streams, contaminating water downstream as far as the oceans. Some also enter groundwater supplies, contaminating well water used by rural residents.

Water Availability

Sustainable farmers handle the twin problems of water availability and water quality separately because they require different techniques and technologies. The key feature in sustainable farming is efficient water use through what is known as drought-proofing. By adding soil organic matter, working to attract a biodiversity of organisms, and maintaining appropriate nutrient levels through techniques such as crop rotation, sustainable farmers already have soils that drain properly and have a high water-holding capacity. This ensures efficient water use. In addition, planting crops that fit local climate and rainfall is essential. These crops might even include heirloom varieties. Also, crops are grown by dry farming, or without irrigation, when possible. Grains are usually dry-farmed, but some vegetables, nuts, and fruits can be as well once they become established.

Greater irrigation efficiency occurs when a larger percentage of irrigation water is taken up by plants and a smaller percentage is lost to evaporation or runoff. Types of irrigation systems include gravity systems, sprinkler irrigation, and trickle or drip irrigation. Gravity irrigation systems distribute water across a field without using pumps. The water flows either across the whole field or into furrows.

◢ **Seeking Solutions**

The 2012 study of the Colorado River basin was part of the Department of the Interior's WaterSMART program, a sustainable water initiative. The study included more than 150 proposals from study participants and the general public suggesting solutions for the water crisis. Proposals included water reuse, desalination, and reducing demand through conservation and efficiency. According to Assistant Secretary for Water and Science Anne Castle, such analyses "pave the way for stakeholders in each basin to come together and determine their own water destiny."[11]

Efficient irrigation systems have leveled or uniform flow to use as little water as possible. In gravity systems, concrete-lined ditches may help efficiency. Other techniques that are helpful but not widely used include irrigating alternate rows or collecting and reusing irrigation runoff. Most gravity systems are only 40 to 65 percent efficient; that is, 35 to 60 percent of the water is not taken up by the plants or soil.[12] Some farmers achieve higher efficiencies of 80 to 90 percent by laser-leveling fields to the exact angle needed for water flow.[13] In laser-leveling, earth-moving equipment smooths a field to the best angle, measured by projecting a laser ahead of the equipment onto the field.

Sprinkler irrigation pumps water and sprays it under pressure through perforated pipes in a specific pattern, similar to rainfall. Sprinklers are designed to deliver water equally to all parts of the field. Pipes may be laid out lengthwise, but most are center-pivot systems that move around in a circle. Sprinkler systems can cover large areas. They have pressure gauges to regulate the rate of water flow, which depends on soil type. Traditional sprinklers spray water from far above. Low-energy precision application (LEPA) systems have small water sprayers that hang down from a water-carrying pipe above. The sprayers decrease evaporation by delivering water at low pressure very close to the ground. Efficiencies for all sprinkler systems range from 50 to 90 percent, with most between 75 and 85 percent.[14] LEPA systems are by far the most efficient.

Trickle or drip irrigation delivers water directly around the plant roots, either on the soil surface or just beneath. It is also called microirrigation because it uses the minimal amount of water required. A network of plastic, perforated pipes is placed throughout the field. The pipes carry water at low flow rates and low pressure, delivering it much more slowly than sprinklers do. It is the most efficient system, at more than 90 percent, and results in the best plant growth.[15]

In a gravity system, siphon tubes carry water from the ditch to the crops.

Good irrigation delivers water to a crop's roots rather than outward, where it will irrigate weed seeds. The type of system depends on the crop. Typical choices are drip irrigation for vegetables, microsprinklers for tree crops, and center-pivot systems for field crops. To be efficient, center-pivot systems must be low-energy and use meters to allow precision application. Overirrigating wastes water and damages plants. It causes too much leaf growth, prevents fruit from growing, and attracts pests. After harvest, overwatered crops rot faster.

Other than the irrigation system, one way to increase efficiency is by irrigation scheduling. This requires either directly measuring the plants' water needs or estimating the rate of water loss and correlating it with plants' needs. Direct measurements involve monitoring leaves or using a soil gauge such as a tensiometer. This instrument measures the suction plant roots must exert to obtain water from soil. During the irrigation season,

Drip irrigation helps prevent water waste by giving crops only what they need.

the water-filled tube of the tensiometer is partially buried in the ground. Its porous tip takes up water from the surrounding soil. A vacuum gauge at the top measures when the soil is dry enough for the farmer to start irrigation.

Estimating water loss is done by collecting weather data and calculating rates of evapotranspiration, or water loss from plants and evaporation. A large-scale scheduled irrigation system in California connects a network of 125 weather stations across the state. The system collects weather data continuously. Evapotranspiration rates are calculated from the weather data using a complex formula and stored in a database than can be accessed via the Internet. In 2010, the database had approximately 6,000 registered users. Scheduled irrigation saves water and improves yields. A study in Saudi Arabia showed improved wheat yields and a 25 percent decrease in water use.[16]

Water Quality

In crop agriculture, a key to maintaining water quality is limiting the runoff of excess nutrients and other dissolved materials. A drainage water management system is designed so water drains into underground pipes and out through one or more outlets. Stopping these outlets with a small dam or other structure holds the water in place. This prevents runoff and keeps the water available for crop use and for recharging the water table. It regulates the water level in the field, either storing water temporarily or allowing it to enter the field as needed. The system retains dissolved nutrients, such as nitrates, improving both yield and downstream water quality.

Buffers, or small areas of permanent vegetation along field edges, can serve many purposes, including water quality management. Native plants provide habitat for wildlife, whose presence increases biodiversity and reduces the need for pesticides. Buffers capture and store water, decreasing

Tensiometers

A tensiometer consists of an airtight, water-filled tube with a porous ceramic tip at the bottom. At the top, it has either a vacuum gauge (left) or a rubber stopper that can be removed to insert a portable vacuum meter (right).

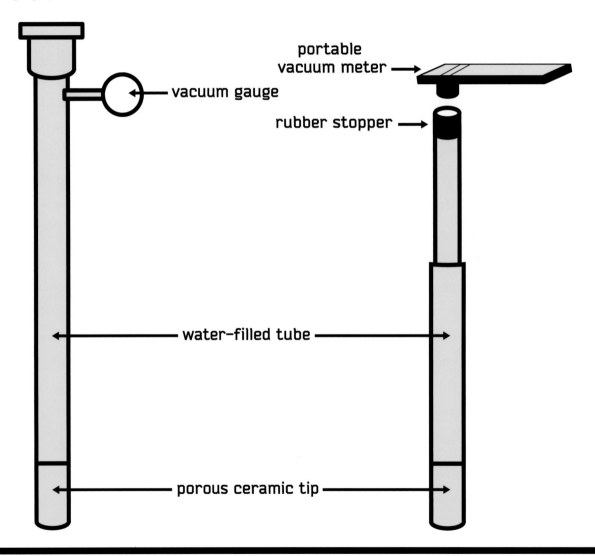

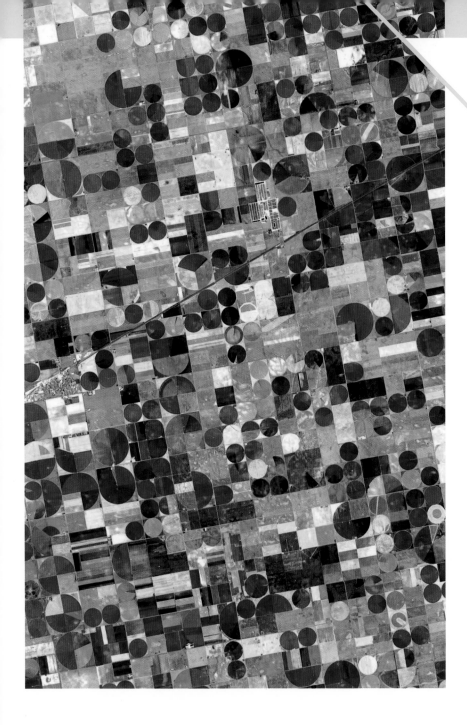

These "crop circles" in Finney County, Kansas, show center-pivot irrigation systems using water from the Ogallala Aquifer.

sediment runoff and retaining soil and dissolved nutrients in the field. In addition, farmers should work to keep and protect wetlands. These areas capture and store runoff, retain and change nutrients into forms plants can use, and break down toxic pollutants. Buffers and wetlands are natural ecosystems that are essential to maintaining water quality in a sustainable farming operation.

SEVEN

SUSTAINABLE ENERGY AND CLIMATE CHANGE

Pinehold Gardens is a 21-acre (8 ha) sustainable vegetable and fruit farm near Milwaukee, Wisconsin. Owners Sandra Raduenz and David Kozlowski installed a solar panel grid in 2005 and added a second in 2008. The two systems provide nearly 100 percent of Pinehold's energy needs for irrigation and refrigeration. The initial system cost approximately $40,000, some of which was paid by government incentives. Raduenz and Kozlowski save thousands of dollars per year on energy bills and sell their excess energy to the local power grid.[1]

Energy efficiency is always a major goal of sustainable agriculture. Although all agriculture uses considerable energy, industrial agriculture's energy use is often excessive compared to sustainable or organic farming. Burning fossil fuels also

Some farmers are beginning to invest in solar panels.

releases large amounts of greenhouse gases, contributing to climate change. Pinehold Gardens increased its sustainability by replacing fossil fuels with solar energy. Other sustainable farmers use wind energy. A few collect farm wastes such as manure to produce methane, which they use as fuel on the farm. But before investing in alternative energy sources, sustainable farmers conserve energy by using it as efficiently as possible.

Most cattle are fed grain. This process consumes large amounts of fossil fuels.

Energy in Industrial Agriculture

Direct energy use in agriculture includes fossil fuels used to run farm machinery, dry crops, care for livestock, and transport goods. It also includes the electricity used to run outbuildings and irrigation pumps. In 2011, direct energy use in industrial agriculture was approximately 63 percent of total energy use. Indirect energy use primarily includes the use of fertilizers and pesticides, some of which are made from fossil fuels. In 2011, it made up 37 percent of the total energy used.[2]

All farms use energy, but many industrial farmers also produce it. They do this by growing corn to produce ethanol. Since the mid-2000s, this biofuel production has increased rapidly due to the passage of federal Renewable Fuel Standards in 2005 and 2007. These laws require corn farmers to produce specified amounts of ethanol for vehicle fuel. In 2012, 4.5 billion bushels of corn, 42 percent of the total produced, were turned into ethanol rather than animal or human food.[3] Growing corn requires massive fossil fuel inputs. For example, many farmers plant corn every year instead of rotating corn and soybeans. Constant corn production requires more fertilizer and therefore more fossil fuels. To produce biofuel, farmers put more acres into corn production and use all crop acres more intensively. Biofuels slightly decrease greenhouse gas emissions, if specific conditions are met—for example, if ethanol plants use energy-efficient natural gas rather than coal.

Greenhouse Gases in Agriculture

Not all greenhouse gases are created equal, and carbon dioxide is not the only important one. Although carbon dioxide makes up by far the greatest percentage of emissions, methane and nitrous oxide trap heat more efficiently. Over a 100-year period, methane traps 23 times more heat in the atmosphere than carbon dioxide, and nitrous oxide traps 296 times more heat. Agriculture contributes 37 percent of US methane emissions and 65 percent of nitrous oxide emissions. Three-fourths of the nitrous oxide emitted by agriculture comes from overusing nitrogen fertilizers. Methane is released from rice production, digestion in cattle and similar animals, and manure storage in CAFO waste lagoons.[5]

Energy Use and Climate Change

Fossil fuel use drives climate change. Using fossil fuels releases vast amounts of greenhouse gases into the environment, including carbon dioxide, methane, and nitrous oxide. These gases trap sunlight energy in the atmosphere, raising the planet's average temperature. This causes more extreme storms, expands deserts in some areas, and increases precipitation and flooding in other areas. Agriculture is causing a significant part of this change—and the changes are coming back to affect agriculture.

According to GRACE Communications Foundation, an environmental organization, agriculture during the 1900s changed from sustainable and locally based to the current "fossil-fuel addicted" system.[4] Today's agriculture emits a significant amount of the world's greenhouse gases.

When soil is covered with growing plants, its carbon and nitrogen are stored and cycled through soil, plants, and bacteria. But when it erodes, this system is torn apart, and the soil releases nitrous oxide and carbon dioxide, both greenhouse gases. Even more nitrous oxide is released when nitrogen fertilizer has been added. Livestock production is also a significant factor. Livestock produce massive

amounts of manure, which releases methane, a major greenhouse gas, as it breaks down. Cattle also produce significant amounts of methane during food digestion, and they release it into the atmosphere during breathing and belching.

Sustainable Farming and Energy Efficiency

Experts worldwide recognize the need to conserve energy in agriculture. A 2011 report by the UN Food and Agriculture Organization (FAO) to the UN Climate Change Conference stressed that, to feed the world's growing population, agriculture must become less dependent on fossil fuels and learn to use energy more wisely.[6] The report stated that approximately one-third of all food production is lost. Energy conservation reduces this loss.

◢ Climate-Smart Agriculture

Climate-smart agriculture (CSA), as defined by the FAO, would fulfill three objectives. First, CSA would lead to a sustainable increase in agricultural productivity to provide worldwide food security. Second, it would make agricultural and food systems more resilient in the face of climate change. Third, CSA would reduce agriculture-based greenhouse gas emissions. Researchers refer to these three objectives as the "triple win" of climate-smart agriculture.[7] In the CSA program, FAO combines its decades of experience with agriculture and food security with methods for decreasing greenhouse gases. Practically speaking, CSA policies are mostly the same as those promoted by the sustainable agriculture movement.

Sustainable farmers cut energy use in two ways. First, they reduce energy use by increasing efficiency; this strategy is easiest and least expensive. Many steps toward energy efficiency cost little and only require modification of existing practices. These include using compost, precision use of fertilizers, fuel-efficient engines, irrigation monitoring, and no-till farming. Another way to cut energy use is to use crop varieties and animal breeds that depend

Using wind and solar power does not put any greenhouse gases into the atmosphere.

less on fossil fuel inputs, such as those adapted to the environmental and climate conditions of a region.

Second, sustainable farmers switch from fossil fuels to alternative energy. Although the initial investment may be large, government incentives are often available, and improvements usually pay for themselves within a few years.

The American Council for an Energy Efficient Economy (ACEEE) focuses on energy use by agricultural facilities rather than crops. It estimated energy efficiency in this area could save the US agriculture sector at least $1 billion per year, with the largest savings occurring in three areas: lighting, motors (especially for irrigation pumping), and on-farm transportation.[8] The most important type of savings depends on the type of farm. Dairy farms can improve energy efficiency in lighting, ventilation, milk-cooling, water heating, and vacuum pumps for milking machines. An energy audit can show where farmers can save the most energy. This can include simple conservation measures such as turning off lights or upgrading to more efficient equipment.

In crop farming, the best way for farmers to be energy efficient is to decrease or eliminate artificial fertilizers and pesticides. This involves precise use of these chemicals, plus techniques already used

▲ Saving Energy in Greenhouses

Three-fourths of the energy used in farm greenhouses is for heating, with smaller amounts used for electricity and vehicles. Some energy-saving methods, such as reducing air leaks, are common sense. Others involve insulating buildings thoroughly and installing highly efficient systems for heating, cooling, and watering. Double insulation is particularly effective. For example, a layer of bubble wrap on the sides, top, and end walls of a greenhouse might be covered with a layer of polyethylene plastic. In cold climates, a single-layered thermal blanket of polypropylene can provide energy savings of 20 to 50 percent.[9]

in soil-building and water conservation, such as the use of cover crops and manures, crop rotation, composting, IPM, and precision farming.

A study of several farm states that depend on irrigation concluded approximately 25 percent of electric energy used in irrigation is wasted.[10] Farmers can decrease energy waste by using more efficient pumps, managing irrigation systems better, matching the pump size to the job, and upgrading to more efficient irrigation systems. On many farms, vehicles cause the greatest energy waste. Improving tractor fuel efficiency and other common-sense measures is a first step. But the most sustainable way to cut energy waste by vehicles is switching to no-till cropping systems.

Alternative Energy for Farms

Three types of alternative energy are used in sustainable farming: wind, solar, and biomass. These energy sources are environmentally friendly because they decrease the farm's dependence on fossil fuels, thereby decreasing pollution and greenhouse gas emissions. They meet all or most of a farm's energy needs, and in many cases provide excess energy to sell for extra income.

The US Department of Energy estimates wind energy could provide 80,000 new jobs and $1.2 billion in revenue for farmers and rural landowners by 2020.[11] Wind power has a long tradition on farms for pumping water and generating electricity. Recently, more farmers in high-wind areas such as the Midwest and West are installing large wind turbines to sell the power they produce to local electric companies or consumers. A single turbine uses less than 0.5 acres (0.2 ha), and farming can continue around turbines.

Solar energy has multiple uses on sustainable farms. In addition to decreasing dependence on fossil fuels, it drastically cuts electricity and heating bills. The most extensive use of solar energy in

agriculture is solar-powered electric fences. Solar energy also heats homes, livestock buildings, and greenhouses. It can heat water for dairy operations, pen cleaning, and home use. Solar electric panels can generate electricity to power pumps and lights.

Biomass is energy produced from organic materials such as manure, trees, crops, and crop residues. Every farm produces raw biomass materials. Crop farms produce crop residues, which the farmer may use for energy or for soil-building and natural fertilizer. Livestock farmers often have more manure than they can use as fertilizer. They can turn the excess into methane biofuel. Fair Oaks Farm, an Indiana dairy farm, does this with the 5 million pounds (2 million kg) of cow manure it generates daily. The biofuel powers their dairy operation, plus a fleet of tractor-trailer trucks that deliver milk to processing facilities. Using biogas for delivery trucks saves an estimated 2 million gallons (7.5 million L) of diesel fuel per year.[12]

◢ Wind Turbines and Corn Growth

Because corn grows best in midwestern plains states where it is windy, people often install wind energy farms on or near corn farms. Scientists are now studying how wind turbines affect corn growth. They think corn might grow better near wind turbines because the wind generated by the turbines supplies the crop with more carbon dioxide, which is needed for photosynthesis. Mixing the air decreases nighttime dew on leaves, possibly resulting in fewer fungal diseases. It might also cause warmer nights and cooler days. Plants would suffer less stress and grow better. But warmer nights might also cause corn plants to lose more energy. Scientists are just beginning research to see if these effects, positive or negative, really occur.

Biomass is often a cash crop. Biomass can produce fuel for vehicles, including tractors, with excess sold to energy companies. Corn is currently the most common crop, but others include prairie grasses such as switchgrass and fast-growing trees such as poplar and willow. As perennial crops, these are all more sustainable than corn. The US Department of Energy estimates tripling the amount

of biomass energy could generate $20 billion in new farm income. The reduction in greenhouse gas emissions would be the equivalent of removing 70 million cars from the road.[13]

Heaps of cow manure can be used as fuel.

EIGHT

INTO THE FUTURE

The Dakota Lakes Research Farm, run by Dr. Dwayne Beck of South Dakota State University, plans to be fossil fuel–neutral by 2026. Not only are fossil fuels the greatest contributor to greenhouse gas emissions, they are also responsible for up to 80 percent of a farm's operating costs.[1] Dr. Beck began by switching to no-till farming, which increased production and cut the farm's fossil fuel use in half.

To eliminate the other half, which still includes some reliance on irrigation and nitrogen fertilizers, he plans to focus on three areas. First, he will add solar panels to an already well-insulated new maintenance building. Second, he will reintroduce cows and other animals to revive the natural nutrient-cycling process; the cows will eat cover crops and crop residues and produce manure to replace fertilizers. Third, he will produce biofuels from soybeans, flax, and canola to heat on-site buildings. Beck says running this sustainable farm will

Canola is used to produce canola oil, an important biofuel.

Floating Solar Farms

The company Forward Thinking Architecture, based in Barcelona, Spain, may have the next big idea in sustainable agriculture. Their solar-powered, automated floating farms are designed to grow vegetables and raise fish in stacked structures located near coastal cities. Fish are farmed on the lowest level, and solar panels power stacks of planting beds. The beds grow vegetables using hydroponics (nutrient-rich water). This vertical, soil-less technology is highly sustainable. Food is grown near where it is needed, and no heavy gasoline-based equipment is required, so fossil fuel use is virtually zero. The pesticide-free farms would not generate agricultural runoff. There would be no crop failures due to droughts, floods, or pest infestations. A farm 656 by 1,148 feet (200 by 350 m) could grow more than 8,152 short tons (7,395 metric tons) of vegetables and 1,703 short tons (1,555 metric tons) of fish per year.[3]

require "less of the stuff you buy and more thinking and more management."[2]

A similar study, the Sunshine Farm Project, was done more than a decade earlier at The Land Institute in Salina, Kansas. Crops provided both animal feed and biodiesel fuel; a solar array produced electricity; and excess electricity was sold to the local energy grid. The goal of the project was to reduce the farm's dependence on fossil fuels and to determine how much of its own energy needs the farm could provide for. Although the farm did achieve a near-zero energy balance, it was not commercially viable.

Floating solar farms, if built, would be able to move to new locations as needed.

The Slow Technology

In the past, agriculture has been a slow-moving discipline; often, it looks as though no change is occurring. After introducing a new crop variety or soil amendment, it has taken years, not days or weeks, to determine how well it works. But many experts believe agriculture is changing rapidly. Chad Kruger, director of the Washington State University Center for Sustaining Agriculture and Natural Resources, says, "We've seen massive changes and adoption of new technology in the past few years as prices were

Gardens for Sustainability

The United Kingdom hopes to expand sustainability and decrease waste by encouraging British consumers to grow food in backyard and community gardens. The country also plans to encourage food businesses and supermarkets to offer more locally grown food. Alabama Extension specialist Kerry Smith also sees a place for home gardens in the United States. "While we can't feed the entire nation with backyard gardens," she says, "these certainly will play a significant role in helping us build this sustainable farm model."[6] The National Center for Appropriate Technology (NCAT), which runs the Small-Scale Intensive Farm Training program (SIFT), notes that sustainable techniques are more suited to small, family-scale farms rather than huge industrial enterprises.

good and there was money to reinvest in agriculture."[4] He says today's farmers are better business managers than in the past, and they are able to make wise decisions about innovations fairly rapidly. This is most obvious in the adoption of new plant varieties.

But in some areas, progress remains slow. The "new" technology of precision agriculture, using GPS technology to localize variations within a field, became available in the mid-1990s. In 2013, a report on precision agriculture in upstate New York said the "systems hold great potential, however further development is needed for their optimal implementation on the farm."[5]

Community gardens can help increase the sustainability of our food sources.

The Spread of Sustainable Farming

Rabobank, a Dutch banking corporation, is a world leader in sustainability and in food and agriculture financing. According to a 2009 Rabobank survey, three-fourths of US farmers are aware of sustainable practices, and approximately 70 percent incorporate some of them. These practices include crop rotation, direct seeding, and minimizing

chemical use. California farmers and ranchers lead in sustainable energy use, particularly solar, and the US dairy industry has set a goal of reducing greenhouse gas emissions by 25 percent by 2020.[7]

Some studies show small-scale organic and sustainable farms release one-half to two-thirds less carbon dioxide for every acre of production than do typical industrial farms. This is because of their reduced use of machines and their reliance on nature rather than synthetic chemicals. These farms appear to use up to one-third less fossil fuel energy and store relatively more carbon in the soil and plants, which keeps the greenhouse gas out of the atmosphere and slows global warming. Rodale Institute estimates that carbon stored in the soil of 10,000 medium-sized organic farms reduces greenhouse gas emissions as much as removing one million cars from the road.[8] However, later studies using different calculations show less obvious benefits related to climate change. Attempts to stem global warming are relatively new, and few studies are available; therefore, the jury is still out on specific results.

But the total acreage of organic farms is miniscule compared to industrial farms. Data released by the USDA for 2011 showed there were approximately 5.38 million acres (2.18 million ha) of certified organic cropland in the United States. This represented less than 1 percent of total US cropland. Total organic sales per year account for slightly more, approximately 4 percent, because many organically grown crops are high-value crops such as garden vegetables and fruits.[9] Also, most organic production comes from a few large organic farms, not from small ones. Organic dairy and poultry products are also on the rise.

"Sustainable farming is not really a destination, but a continuum," says Chad Kruger. "Even the most sustainable farm today will likely not be considered sustainable in 20 years without changing more."[10] Farmers use a variety of techniques—some sustainable and some not. It is likely this continuum will

Foods with the organic label must meet strict guidelines from the USDA.

shift more and more in the direction of sustainable farming practices as studies show the benefits of sustainability.

Balancing Sustainability with Large-Scale Production

Many agricultural experts are asking whether sustainability can be balanced with large-scale farming. By 2050, the world population is expected to be 9.5 billion, up from 7.2 billion in 2015.[11] Experts estimate we will need 50 percent more food, while water and fossil fuel energy will become less available.[12]

Some American agricultural extension agents, county employees who work with farmers to improve production, suggest modern industrial agriculture is necessary because it produces cheap food. They argue more expensive sustainable techniques will raise food prices, adversely

affecting millions of people. Professor John Beddington, chief science adviser to the British government, says feeding growing populations will require producing more crops on less land and greater use of emerging technologies such as genetically modified foods and nanotechnology. Others have said feeding the world with organic farming would require much more land and all forests would have to be cut.

Industrial farms typically have more acreage and machines than small organic and sustainable farms.

But some organizations strongly reject these arguments. The Worldwatch Institute, a nonprofit organization that researches sustainable living, says converting to organic farming lowers yields in the first few years, but as soil and biodiversity recover, yields increase with them. The group also observes that the gap in yields between organic and industrial farming is greatest in developed countries, where unsustainable levels of fertilizers and pesticides are used. The gap is least in the world's poorest, hungriest nations.

In a 2014 study, British scientists argued organic agriculture is much more productive than previously thought. They found organic yields were only 19.2 percent lower than conventional yields. They also said this gap could be reduced to 8 percent with existing techniques, especially increasing crop rotation and multicropping, or growing several crops in the same field.[13] Yields of organic legumes such as beans and peas already equal industrial agriculture yields. The British scientists further point out that switching to sustainable methods will soon be a necessity, not a choice, because industrial agriculture is so unsustainable. They recommend more research to develop better organic, sustainable techniques.

But at present, "modern" organic farming is very new—only a few decades old—and too little information is available to make definite statements about its long-term viability. Some of the

longest-running organic farms are now having difficulty with diseases, weeds, and insects. After a certain time, yields begin to drop to pre-industrial levels.

Despite limited information, organic, sustainable farming is being implemented around the world. Approximately one-third of organically farmed land is located in developing regions.[14] The three countries with the greatest amounts of organically farmed land are Australia, Argentina, and China. There are also large amounts in Oceania, Europe, and Latin America. Small-scale farming provides food and economic stability for underdeveloped regions. It incorporates key features of sustainable agriculture, including combining plant and animal agriculture into single farms to maintain biodiversity and build soil. The greatest barrier to implementing this strategy, according to UN member Olivier de Schutter, is convincing policymakers that small-scale farming is better than standard industrial methods.

Thus, for the near future, it appears industrial agriculture will continue to reign supreme in the United States and around the world. But sustainable agriculture advocates are making inroads by implementing small-scale sustainable farming and by introducing sustainable techniques into industrial farming operations.

High-Tech Sustainability

In the past several decades, two hot new agricultural technologies have surfaced: biotechnology and nanotechnology. Biotechnology—the use of genetic modification to produce new crop varieties with special characteristics—started earlier and is now spreading rapidly. New GM varieties will continue to appear, but they are often not sustainable. This technology has promise, but it is now in the testing phase, where questions about its effectiveness and sustainability must be answered with long-term,

detailed studies. Nanotechnology has only begun to appear. It too could transform agriculture for the better, but again, only if properly applied. For example, proposed applications such as nanosensors to detect diseases or nutrient deficiencies could make precision agriculture even more efficient.

An even newer application of nanotechnology is the nanocatalyst. A catalyst is a structure or substance that changes the rate of a chemical reaction. Nanocatalysts are extremely tiny catalysts, usually measuring ten nanometers or less. Many of them contain elements such as aluminum, iron, or silver. Nanocatalysts in agriculture may increase pesticide efficiency, so lower doses can be used. Others may reduce pollution, clean up existing pollution, or help develop alternative energy sources. Still others will help plants absorb nutrients, combat viral diseases, or monitor the quality of agricultural produce. Many nanotechnology applications are likely to take decades to develop, and because the technology is so new, no one is certain what applications will be available

◢ The Fieldprint Calculator

An organization called Field to Market: The Alliance for Sustainable Agriculture has developed a downloadable software program that helps sustainable farmers determine just how sustainable their operations are. The user enters data about his or her farming operation. The Fieldprint Calculator determines the farm's performance in sustainability areas including:

» Land use

» Conservation

» Soil carbon

» Irrigation water use

» Water quality

» Energy use

» Greenhouse gas emissions

The farmer can see graphs of the farm's performance, determine how specific changes will influence sustainability, and compare the farm's performance against local, state, and national averages.

*Scientists continue working on
sustainable varieties of GM crops.*

first. Also, at this point, no one knows what impacts nanotechnology will have on food production, humans, or the environment.

In the 2000s, sustainable farmers hope to turn agriculture around. They hope to move from the 1900s' unsustainable fossil fuel–based methods toward a sustainable system that works with, rather than against, nature. But they are not going backward. They hope tomorrow's sustainable agriculture will reclaim some of the best techniques of preindustrial agriculture and combine them with new technologies, including alternative energy, biotechnology, nanotechnology, and other future discoveries. More research is needed, but over the next decades, as world food security becomes increasingly vital and effects of climate change snowball, we may, out of necessity, see agriculture transformed—into sustainable agriculture.

ESSENTIAL FACTS

Key Discoveries

» **Alternative energy technologies:** Adaptation of alternative energy technologies such as solar, wind, and biomass decreases fossil fuel use on farms.

» **Composting and soil building:** Indian farmers developed principles of composting and soil building.

» **Genetically modified seeds and animals:** Genetically modified seeds and animals produce new crops with improved productivity, better nutritional quality, or better resistance to pests.

» **GPS and GIS:** GPS and GIS technologies provide images of crop growth in various parts of a field and make precision agriculture possible.

» **Integrated pest management:** Integrated pest management replaces massive pesticide use.

» **Nanotechnology:** Use of nanotechnology enables the development of sensors and delivery systems for agriculture.

» **No-till and low-till:** No-till and low-till methods enable farmers to maintain soil health and decrease erosion.

Key Players

» **Albert Howard:** Sir Albert Howard, a British botanist, writes the 1940 book *An Agricultural Testament*, outlining sustainable agriculture principles, including composting and natural pest control.

» **John Ikerd:** Dr. John Ikerd of the University of Missouri defines the term *sustainable agriculture* and is a key developer of the field.

» **Rachel Carson:** Rachel Carson writes the 1962 book *Silent Spring*, which warns of pesticide dangers.

Key Tools and Technologies

» **Genetic modification:** New crop varieties are developed by transferring genes from other species into the modified crop species.

» **Nanotechnology:** Tiny structures, often measuring less than 100 nanometers, are used to precisely measure soil or control inputs to a field.

» **Precision agriculture:** GPS and GIS technologies enable farmers to tailor amounts of seed, fertilizer, pesticide, or other materials needed in various parts of a field.

Future Outlook

Worsening world problems such as climate change, soil depletion, water scarcity, population growth, and decreased world food security may force changes in agriculture. Technologies such as drip irrigation will enable farmers to conserve water, while renewable energy sources such as wind and solar will prevent large amounts of greenhouse gases from entering the atmosphere. GM crop varieties will likely increase. Nanosensors and particles may enable slow fertilizer release.

Quote

"Soils are a form of technology. . . . They perform useful work transforming one group of substances into another."

—*Dr. Rachel Armstrong*

GLOSSARY

acequia

An irrigation ditch or canal, community-operated and based on the concept of equal and fair use of water.

aquifer

A permeable, or spongelike, region of underground rock that stores groundwater.

arable

Fertile, or able to grow crops.

CAFO

A confined animal feeding operation, also called a factory farm; a facility in which food animals are kept in highly confined conditions and fed a high-calorie diet plus hormones and antibiotics.

calorie

A unit of energy, used in describing the amount of energy present in food; specifically, the amount of energy needed to raise the temperature of 1 gram of water 1°C.

compost

A type of natural fertilizer made from decayed organic matter, such as dead leaves, grass clippings, manure, and vegetable remains.

conservation tillage

A type of farming in which tillage is limited; minimal tilling is designed to prevent or decrease erosion and maintain soil health.

desalination

The process of taking salt out of water.

fossil fuels

Energy sources based on coal, oil, or natural gas. These fuels were formed millions of years ago from ancient plant and animal remains.

genetic modification (GM)

Changing the genetic information in a cell to make new crop plants having desired characteristics.

groundwater

Water stored in underground aquifers and made available for use by drilling wells.

ion

An atom that has an electric charge; this occurs when the number of electrons is not equal to the number of protons.

monoculture

Growing a single crop on the same piece of land year after year, resulting in a continuing need for fertilizers and pesticides.

mulch

A covering, such as leaves or wood chips, placed over soil to conserve moisture and reduce the growth of weeds.

nanotechnology

The assembly and manipulation of structures at the level of atoms or molecules to carry out agricultural functions.

no-till farming

A system of farming in which land is not plowed and seeds are injected through existing crop residue, resulting in reduced erosion and preservation of nutrients.

permaculture

A sustainable agricultural system composed of perennial or self-perpetuating plants, promoted as an alternative to monocultures.

tilling

Turning over arable land by plowing or other means.

topsoil

The top layer of soil, where most nutrients, organic matter, and organisms are found.

ADDITIONAL RESOURCES

Selected Bibliography

Committee on Twenty-First Century Systems Agriculture, Board on Agriculture and Natural Resources, Division on Earth and Life Sciences. *Toward Sustainable Agricultural Systems in the 21st Century*. Washington, DC: National Academies, 2010. Print.

Feenstra, Gail. "What Is Sustainable Agriculture?" *Agricultural Sustainability Institute*. University of California Regents, n.d. Web. 20 Apr. 2015.

Kleppel, Gary S. *The Emergent Agriculture: Farming, Sustainability, and the Return of the Local Economy*. Gabriola, BC: New Society, 2014. Print.

Thistlethwaite, Rebecca. *Farms with a Future: Creating and Growing a Sustainable Farm Business*. White River Junction, VT: Chelsea Green, 2013. Print.

Further Readings

Fox, Thomas J. *Urban Farming: Sustainable City Living in Your Backyard, in Your Community, and in the World*. Irvine, CA: Hobby Farm, 2011. Print.

Johanson, Paula. *Jobs in Sustainable Agriculture*. New York: Rosen, 2010. Print.

Owings, Lisa. *Sustainable Agriculture*. Minneapolis: Abdo, 2013. Print.

Websites

To learn more about Cutting-Edge Science and Technology, visit **booklinks.abdopublishing.com**. These links are routinely monitored and updated to provide the most current information available.

For More Information

For more information on this subject, contact or visit the following organizations:

Field to Market: The Alliance for Sustainable Agriculture

777 N Capitol Street NE, Suite 803
Washington, DC 20002
202-417-3874
https://www.fieldtomarket.org/

This organization is a diverse group of agriculture, food, and conservation organizations banding together to define, measure, and advance sustainability in the production of food, fuel, and fiber.

The Food Project

10 Lewis Street
Lincoln, MA 01773
781-259-8621
http://thefoodproject.org/what-we-do

This sustainable farm in Massachusetts works with teenagers and volunteers, teaching sustainable farming, food production, and personal and social change through community action.

National Young Farmers Coalition

P.O. Box 1074
Hudson, NY 12534
518-643-3564
http://www.youngfarmers.org/land-and-jobs/

This organization lists, by region, many opportunities for internships, apprenticeships, and jobs for young people interested in sustainable farming.

SOURCE NOTES

Chapter 1. Defining Sustainable Agriculture

1. "What Is Sustainable Agriculture?" *Sustainable Agriculture Research and Education*. Sustainable Agriculture Research and Education, 2010. Web. 21 July 2015.

2. Ibid.

3. Ibid.

4. Ibid.

5. Mary V. Gold. "Sustainable Agriculture: Information Access Tools." *USDA National Agricultural Library*. United States Department of Agriculture, 29 June 2015. Web. 21 July 2015.

Chapter 2. Why We Need Sustainable Agriculture

1. John Ikerd. "The Future of Food: Sustainable Agriculture Is Not Optional." *University of Missouri*. University of Missouri, 24 Apr. 2012. Web. 21 July 2015.

2. "Honey Bee Health and Colony Collapse Disorder." *USDA Agricultural Research Service*. United States Department of Agriculture, 13 May 2015. Web. 19 Mar. 2015.

3. "Fossil Fuel and Energy Use." *Sustainable Table*. New York University, n.d. Web. 21 July 2015.

4. "Farming: Wasteful Water Use." *WWF*. WWF, n.d. Web. 21 July 2015.

5. Case Adams. "What Do Pesticides, Herbicides, and Antibiotics Have in Common?" *GreenMedInfo*. GreenMedInfo, 17 July 2013. Web. 18 Mar. 2015.

6. Bob Hartzler, et al. "Glyphosate, Weeds, and Crops: Understanding Glyphosate to Increase Performance." *The Education Store*. Purdue University, 19 Dec. 2006. Web. 21 July 2015.

7. Mary V. Gold. "Sustainable Agriculture: Information Access Tools." *USDA National Agricultural Library*. United States Department of Agriculture, 29 June 2015. Web. 21 July 2015.

Chapter 3. Sustainable Soil

1. Rebecca Thistlethwaite. *Farms with a Future: Creating and Growing a Sustainable Farm Business*. White River Junction, VT: Chelsea Green, 2012. Print. 122–123.

2. Ibid.

3. Helmut Kohnke and D.P. Franzmeier. *Soil Science Simplified*. 4th ed. Prospect Heights, IL: Waveland, 1995. Print. 3, 5.

4. "Carbon to Nitrogen Ratios in Cropping Systems." *USDA Natural Resources Conservation Service*. United States Department of Agriculture, Jan. 2011. Web. 21 July 2015.

5. "Soil Erosion." *National Department of Agriculture, Directorate Agricultural Land and Resources Management*. National Department of Agriculture, 1999. Web. 21 July 2015.

6. "Soil Erosion and Degradation." *WWF*. WWF, n.d. Web. 21 July 2015.

7. "Carbon to Nitrogen Ratios in Cropping Systems." *USDA Natural Resources Conservation Service*. United States Department of Agriculture, Jan. 2011. Web. 21 July 2015.

8. "Farming in the 21st Century: A Practical Approach to Improve Soil Health." *USDA Natural Resources Conservation Service*. United States Department of Agriculture, Sep. 2010. Web. 21 July 2015.

9. Board on Agriculture and Natural Resources. *Toward Sustainable Agricultural Systems in the 21st Century*. Washington, DC: National Academies, 2010. Print. 86–90.

10. Rachel Armstrong. "Why Synthetic Soil Holds the Key to a Sustainable Future." *The Guardian*. Guardian News and Media, 17 Jan. 2014. Web. 21 July 2015.

Chapter 4. Chemicals and Precision Agriculture

1. Board on Agriculture and Natural Resources. *Toward Sustainable Agricultural Systems in the 21st Century*. Washington, DC: National Academies, 2010. Print. 133–134.

2. Karl Tupper. "At Long Last: EPA Releases Pesticide Use Statistics." *Ground Truth*. Pesticide Action Network North America, 22 Feb. 2011. Web. 21 July 2015.

3. Elena Day. "WHO Says Roundup Is 'Probably' Cancer-Causing." *Crozet Gazette*. Crozet Gazette, 3 Apr. 2015. Web. 21 July 2015.

4. Eliza Grizwold. "How 'Silent Spring' Ignited the Environmental Movement." *New York Times Magazine*. New Your Times Company, 21 Sep. 2012. Web. 21 July 2015.

5. Ioulia Fenton. "Five Sustainable and Fascinatingly Fun Pest Management Techniques." *Nourishing the Planet*. Nourishing the Planet, 4 Sep. 2012. Web. 21 July 2015.

6. Ibid.

Chapter 5. Seeds and Biotechnology

1. Dan Charles. "The Family Peach Farm That Became a Symbol of the Food Revolution." *NPR*. NPR, 14 Mar. 2015. Web. 21 July 2015.

2. "New Report Finds Farmers Harmed by Decline in Nation's Public Seed Supply." *National Sustainable Agriculture Coalition*. National Sustainable Agriculture Coalition, 21 Oct. 2014. Web. 21 July 2015.

3. Ibid.

4. Svalbard Global Seed Vault." *Crop Trust*. Crop Trust, n.d. Web. 21 July 2015.

5. "The Sustainability of Biotechnology." *Biotechnology Industry Organization*. Biotechnology Industry Organization, n.d. Web. 21 July 2015.

6. "The Impact of Genetically Engineered Crops on Farm Sustainability in the United States." *National Academy of Sciences*. National Academies, 2010. Web. 21 July 2015.

7. "Is GM Agriculture Sustainable?" *Barilla Center for Food and Nutrition*. Barilla Center for Food and Nutrition, 2010. Web. 21 July 2015.

8. Wayne Weiseman. "Wes Jackson and the Land Institute." *The Permaculture Project*. The Permaculture Project, 21 Oct. 2009. Web. 21 July 2015.

Chapter 6. Sustainable Water

1. Wochit News. "California Snowpack Wilts to Shocking All-Time Record Low." *YouTube*. YouTube, 1 Apr. 2015. Web. 21 July 2015.

2. "Top Story: Governor Brown Directs First Ever Statewide Mandatory Water Reductions." *California Drought*. State of California, 1 Apr. 2015. Web. 21 July 2015.

3. Mark Bittman. "Everyone Eats There." *New York Times Magazine.* New York Times Company, 10 Oct. 2012. Web. 21 July 2015.

4. Dennis Dimick. "If You Think the Water Crisis Can't Get Worse, Wait Until the Aquifers Are Drained." *National Geographic.* National Geographic Society, 21 Aug. 2014. Web. 21 July 2015.

5. Ibid.

6. "Water Quality." Grace Communications Foundation. Grace Communications Foundation, n.d. Web. 21 July 2015.

7. "Climate-Smart Agriculture 2015." *Global Science Conference.* Cirad, n.d. Web. 21 July 2015.

8. Board on Agriculture and Natural Resources. *Toward Sustainable Agricultural Systems in the 21st Century.* Washington, DC: National Academies, 2010. Print. 59.

9. Ibid.

10. "Secretary Salazar Releases Colorado River Basin Study Projecting Major Imbalances in Water Supply and Demand." *US Department of the Interior.* US Department of the Interior, n.d. Web. 21 July 2015.

11. Tovin Lapan. "Department of Interior Releases Colorado River Study." *Las Vegas Sun.* Las Vegas Sun, 12 Dec. 2012. Web. 21 July 2015.

12. Board on Agriculture and Natural Resources. *Toward Sustainable Agricultural Systems in the 21st Century.* Washington, DC: National Academies, 2010. Print. 112–113.

13. Moriah Costa. "From Laser-Leveled Fields to Drip Irrigation, Farms Stretch Water They Have." *Cronkite News.* Cronkite News, 11 Apr. 2014. Web. 21 July 2015.

14. Board on Agriculture and Natural Resources. *Toward Sustainable Agricultural Systems in the 21st Century.* Washington, DC: National Academies, 2010. Print. 113–114.

15. C. Wilson and M. Bauer. "Drip Irrigation for Home Gardens." *Colorado State University Extension.* Colorado State University Extension, July 2014. Web. 21 July 2015.

16. Board on Agriculture and Natural Resources. *Toward Sustainable Agricultural Systems in the 21st Century.* Washington, DC: National Academies, 2010. Print. 112.

Chapter 7. Sustainable Energy and Climate Change

1. Irene M. Xiarchos and Brian Vick. "Solar Energy Use in US Agriculture Overview and Policy Issues." *US Department of Agriculture.* US Department of Agriculture, Apr. 2011. Web. 21 July 2015.

2. Jayson Beckman, Allison Borchers, and Carol A. Jones. "Agriculture's Supply and Demand for Energy and Energy Products." *US Department of Agriculture.* US Department of Agriculture, May 2013. Web. 21 July 2015.

3. Ibid.

4. "Agriculture, Energy, and Climate Change: Taking a Bite out of Climate Change." *Grace Communications Foundation.* Grace Communications Foundation, n.d. Web. 21 July 2015.

5. Ibid.

6. "'Energy-Smart' Agriculture Needed to Escape Fossil Fuel Trap." *Food and Agriculture Organization of the United Nations.* Food and Agriculture Organization of the United Nations, 29 Nov. 2011. Web. 21 July 2015.

7. "Energy Efficiency in Agriculture." *Washington State Department of Agriculture*. Washington State Department of Agriculture, 11 May 2012. Web. 21 July 2015.

8. "Greenhouse Energy Conservation Checklist." *Center for Agriculture, Food, and the Environment*. University of Massachusetts Amherst, May 2005. Web. 21 July 2015.

9. "Energy Efficiency in Agriculture." *Washington State Department of Agriculture*. Washington State Department of Agriculture, 11 May 2012. Web. 21 July 2015.

10. "Renewable Energy and Agriculture: A Natural Fit." *Union of Concerned Scientists*. Union of Concerned Scientists, n.d. Web. 21 July 2015.

11. Ibid.

12. Steven Yaccino. "Dairy Finds a Way to Let Cows Power Trucks." *New York Times*. New York Times Company, 27 Mar. 2013. Web. 21 July 2015.

13. "Renewable Energy and Agriculture: A Natural Fit." *Union of Concerned Scientists*. Union of Concerned Scientists, n.d. Web. 21 July 2015.

Chapter 8. Into the Future

1. Bob Schmidt. "The Way of the Future: Fossil-Fuel Free Farms." *Farm Credit Services of America*. Farm Credit Services of America, 11 Mar. 2014. Web. 21 July 2015.

2. Ibid.

3. Zi-Ann Lum. "This Floating Solar Farm May One Day Grow 8,000 Tons of Veggies Every Year." *Huffington Post Canada*. Huffington Post, 2 June 2015. Web. 21 July 2015.

4. Chad Kruger. Personal communication. 29 May 2015.

5. Pamela Espinosa de los Monteros and Daniel Ochs. "Precision Agriculture in Upstate NY: An Overview." *Association for Information Science and Technology*. Association for Information Science and Technology, n.d. Web. 21 July 2015.

6. Jim Langcuster. "Can We Balance Sustainability with Large-Scale Farming?" *Southeast Farm Press*. Penton, 11 Feb. 2010. Web. 21 July 2015.

7. "Sustainable Practices in Place at 70% of US Farms." *Environmental Leader*. Business Sector Media, 22 Apr. 2009. Web. 21 July 2015.

8. "Agriculture, Energy, and Climate Change: Taking a Bite out of Climate Change." *Grace Communications Foundation*. Grace Communications Foundation, n.d. Web. 21 July 2015.

9. "Organic Production: Overview." *USDA Economic Research Service*. United States Department of Agriculture. 24 Oct. 2013. Web. 21 July 2015.

10. Chad Kruger. Personal communication. 29 May 2015.

11. Jim Langcuster. "Can We Balance Sustainability with Large-Scale Farming?" *Southeast Farm Press*. Penton, 11 Feb. 2010. Web. 21 July 2015.

12. Ibid.

13. Tom Bawden. "Organic Farming Can Feed the World if Done Right, Scientists Claim." *The Independent*. The Independent, 10 Dec. 2014. Web. 21 July 2015.

14. "Organic Industrial Agriculture." *Mission 2014: Feeding the World*. Massachusetts Institute of Technology, n.d. Web. 21 July 2015.

INDEX

About the Author

Carol Hand has a PhD in zoology with a specialization in ecology and environmental science. Before becoming a science writer, she taught college, wrote for standardized testing companies, and developed multimedia science curricula. She has written more than 25 books for young people on topics including soils, climate change, urban gardens, biomass energy, and environmental engineering.